The MAILBOX®

The Education Center®

Sounds Like Fun

Phenomenal Phonics®

S0-AAD-988

Ideas, Centers, and Reproducibles for Beginning Consonants, Blends, & Digraphs; Word Families; Short & Long Vowels

- Phonemic Awareness
- Letter Recognition
- Letter-Sound Association

- Spelling Long Vowels
- Reading

Written and Illustrated by Lucia Kemp Henry

Managing Editor: Allison E. Ward

Editorial Team: Becky S. Andrews, Kimberley Bruck, Karen P. Shelton, Diane Badden, Thad H. McLaurin, Karen A. Brudnak, Sarah Hamblet, Hope Rodgers, Dorothy C. McKinney

Production Team: Lisa K. Pitts, Pam Crane, Rebecca Saunders, Jennifer Tipton Cappoen, Chris Curry, Sarah Foreman, Theresa Lewis Goode, Clint Moore, Greg D. Rieves, Barry Slate, Donna K. Teal, Zane Williard, Tazmen Carlisle, Irene Harvley-Felder, Amy Kirtley-Hill, Kristy Parton, Cathy Edwards Simrell, Lynette Dickerson, Mark Rainey, Ivy L. Koonce

www.themailbox.com

Manufactured in the United States
10 9 8 7 6 5 4 3 2 1

Table of

Contents

Using Phenomenal

This book contains

- 36 inspiring ideas

- 31 full-color centers that are ready to laminate and use

- 31 reproducible cut-and-paste sorting activities

- 39 reproducible miniposters

Use the miniposters (pages 155–168) as learning aids. In a snap, make

display cards
(blends display shown)

word wall headers
(word family word wall shown)

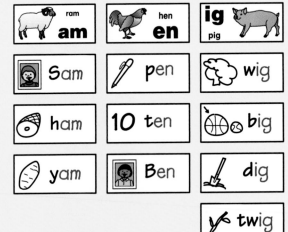

booklet covers
(ee word booklet and i_e word booklet shown)

Phonics®

Sounds Like Fun

Teach with fun, purposeful ideas.

Choose one or more ideas for teaching or reinforcing letter-sound relationships, word families, or spellings. Then have children

sing   suggest   listen   write

move   play   chant   spell

observe   collaborate   sort   discuss

Reinforce with ready-to-go centers.

Show children how to complete a center. For ease, each center in this book is completed in a similar way.

On the center mat, place only the picture cards whose names match the key words.

Reinforce with reproducibles.

Use the cut-and-glue reproducibles for confidence-building practice.

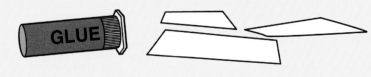

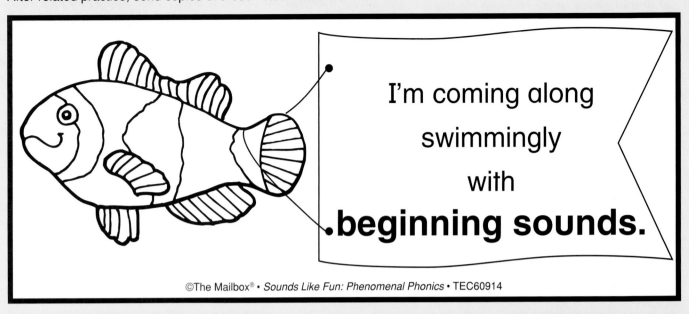

I'm coming along swimmingly with **beginning sounds.**

wish dish fish

It's fun to read **word families.**

Let's read some together.

crab cab tab slab lab

Spelling long vowels is tricky!

But I'm learning how to do it.

Ask me to spell the picture words.

Initial Consonants

Contents

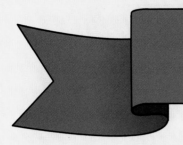

An Animal Anthem

Children love critters so much that they will be naturally interested in associating animal names with beginning consonants. Sing this song to introduce or review this section's 15 beginning consonants and their associated animal keywords.

(sung to the tune of "The Farmer in the Dell")

Oh, *bear* begins with *b.*
Oh, *bear* begins with *b.*
/B/, /b/, /b/, /b/, /b/, /b/.
Oh, *bear* begins with *b.*
Repeat this verse, making appropriate substitutions for cat, dog, fox, goat, horse, mouse, newt, pig, seal, *and* wolf. *Continue with the additional verses below.*

Oh, *lion* starts with *l.*
Oh, *lion* starts with *l.*
/L/, /l/, /l/, /l/, /l/, /l/.
Oh, *lion* starts with *l.*
Repeat this verse, making appropriate substitutions for raccoon *and* turtle.

Koala starts with *k.*
Koala starts with *k.*
/K/, /k/, /k/, /k/, /k/, /k/.
Koala starts with *k.*

What Letter Does It Start With?

Once your children have been introduced to the troupe of initial-consonant animals in this section, get a quick reading on their letter-sound association skills with this instant activity. If you have individual chalkboards or whiteboards, distribute them along with writing instruments. Otherwise, have children write their responses on paper. Call out each of these animal names in turn: bear, cat, fox, goat, horse, koala, mouse, newt, pig, seal, wolf, dog, lion, raccoon, turtle. As you name an animal, have each child write its initial consonant. As children write, observe their answers. Then discuss the letter they wrote and why they chose it. (Ask children using chalkboards or whiteboards to erase their answers before the next animal is named.) Continue this routine for all 15 animals.

Consonants

Letter-Sound Roundup

Get your children on their feet for a shindig that will make letter-sound association a real treat. To prepare, choose four of the letter-animal pairings from this section. You might start, for example, with *t* for *turtle, r* for *raccoon, b* for *bear,* and *g* for *goat.* For each of the four featured letters, gather enough letter cards, die-cut letters, or magnetic letters for one quarter of the class. To begin the game, have children stand in a circle. Give each child a letter and ask him to say its name and sound. Explain that as you sing the first verse together, children holding letters that represent the beginning sound in the animal name are to take two giant steps into the center of the circle for the roundup. During the second verse, have them hold their letters way up high. Have these children return to their original places in the circle and continue singing the song, substituting *raccoon, bear,* and *goat* for *turtle.*

(sung to the tune of "Short'nin' Bread")

Every critter's ready for the
Roundup, roundup!
Come on, all you [turtles],
It's roundup time!

Every [turtle]'s right here in the
Roundup, roundup!
Show your letters, [turtles].
It's roundup time!

Lions and Turtles and Bears! Oh, My!

After students are familiar with the animal illustrations on the center mats and skill sheets in this section, put a creative flair in consonant review with this quick and easy poster project. To prepare a poster for each initial consonant you wish to feature, use a wide black marker to write a consonant in the upper left corner of a 12" x 18" sheet of white construction paper. Assign several students to work, in turn, on each poster and emphasize which animal corresponds to the letter. On each poster, have the assigned students take turns drawing, coloring, and labeling pictures of the matching animal. Then display the posters around the room, adding paper posts and grass, if you wish, so that the posters resemble signs.

Initial Consonants

Magnetic Matchups

Use this letter-and-picture matching center to provide your youngsters with more reinforcement fun. Reproduce and cut out construction paper copies of the picture cards on pages 12, 16, 20, 24, and 28. Select one picture card to match each of the 15 consonants in this section (*m, s, p, t, n, g, b, r, k, w, l, f, h, d,* and *c),* reserving the extra pictures for use with "Consonant Concentration" on this page. Stock a center with the picture cards, a small magnetboard, and a letter magnet to match the beginning letter in the name of each picture. Encourage each child visiting the center to use a letter magnet to post the corresponding picture on the board.

Consonant Concentration

Capture the interest of your little ones with this Consonant Concentration game. Cut out 15 two-inch squares of construction paper. Use a marker to label each one with one of these consonants: *m, s, p, t, n, g, b, r, k, w, l, f, h, d,* or *c.* Prepare a picture card to match each consonant square. (If you prepared the center described in "Magnetic Matchups," above, simply select one of the remaining picture cards to match each consonant square.) To play with a small group of children, place all 30 cards facedown on a tabletop. Have children take turns flipping two cards per turn to find a letter-picture match. Children who find matches hold on to those cards as play continues. When all the matches have been located, everyone's a winner!

Consonants: *m, s, p*

Consonants: *m, s, p*

Consonants: *m, s, p*

Consonants: *m, s, p*

Consonants: *m, s, p*

Consonants: *m, s, p*

Consonants: *m, s, p*

Consonants: *m, s, p*

Consonants: *m, s, p*

Consonants: *m, s, p*

Consonants: *m, s, p*

Consonants: *m, s, p*

Use these cards with the center mat on page 13.

1. Before using page 13, photocopy page 14 for later use.
2. If desired, laminate the center mat (page 13) and the cards.
3. Cut out the cards.
4. To use, a child turns all the cards full-color side up on a tabletop.

5. The child chooses a picture card and names the picture. He places it beside the picture on the mat that has a matching beginning sound. He continues in this way until each space on the center mat is filled.
6. The child names the pictures in each set, listening to confirm that all the pictures begin with the same sound. He flips each card to check his work.

These cards may also be used with "Magnetic Matchups" and "Consonant Concentration" on page 10.

Begins Like Seal

Begins Like Mouse

Begins Like Pig

Begins Like Mouse, Pig, or Seal

Cut. Glue.

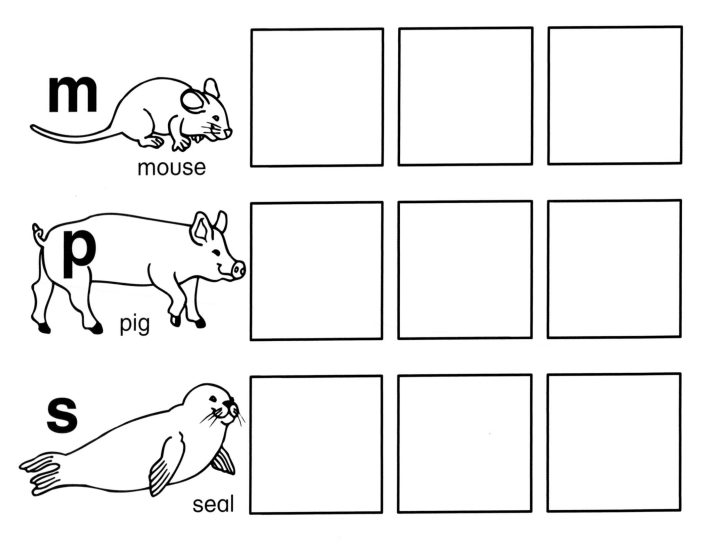

m
mouse

p
pig

s
seal

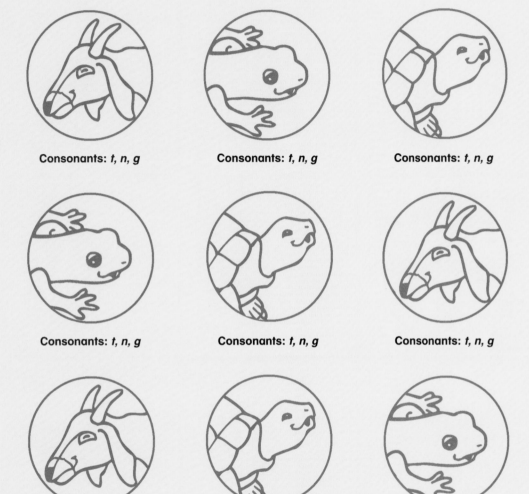

Consonants: *t, n, g*   Consonants: *t, n, g*   Consonants: *t, n, g*

Consonants: *t, n, g*   Consonants: *t, n, g*   Consonants: *t, n, g*

Consonants: *t, n, g*   Consonants: *t, n, g*   Consonants: *t, n, g*

Consonants: *t, n, g*   Consonants: *t, n, g*   Consonants: *t, n, g*

Use these cards with the center mat on page 17.

1. Before using page 17, photocopy page 18 for later use.
2. If desired, laminate the center mat (page 17) and the cards.
3. Cut out the cards.
4. To use, a child turns all the cards full-color side up on a tabletop.
5. The child chooses a picture card and names the picture. She places it beside the picture on the mat that has a matching beginning sound. She continues in this way until each space on the center mat is filled.
6. The child names the pictures in each set, listening to confirm that all the pictures begin with the same sound. She flips each card to check her work.

These cards may also be used with "Magnetic Matchups" and "Consonant Concentration" on page 10.

Begins Like Goat

Begins Like Newt

Begins Like Turtle

Begins Like Turtle, Newt, or Goat

Cut. Glue.

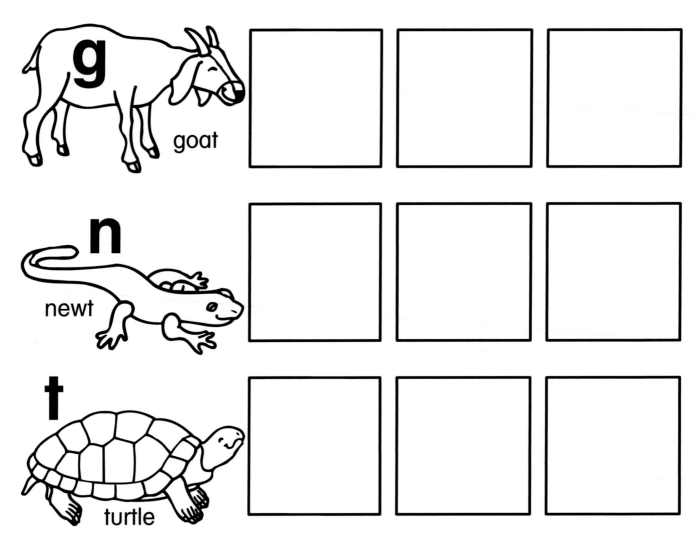

Consonants: *b, r, k*

Consonants: *b, r, k*

Consonants: *b, r, k*

Consonants: *b, r, k*

Consonants: *b, r, k*

Consonants: *b, r, k*

Consonants: *b, r, k*

Consonants: *b, r, k*

Consonants: *b, r, k*

Consonants: *b, r, k*   Consonants: *b, r, k*   Consonants: *b, r, k*

Use these cards with the center mat on page 21.

1. Before using page 21, photocopy page 22 for later use.
2. If desired, laminate the center mat (page 21) and the cards.
3. Cut out the cards.
4. To use, a child turns all the cards full-color side up on a tabletop.

5. The child chooses a picture card and names the picture. He places it beside the picture on the mat that has a matching beginning sound. He continues in this way until each space on the center mat is filled.
6. The child names the pictures in each set, listening to confirm that all the pictures begin with the same sound. He flips each card to check his work.

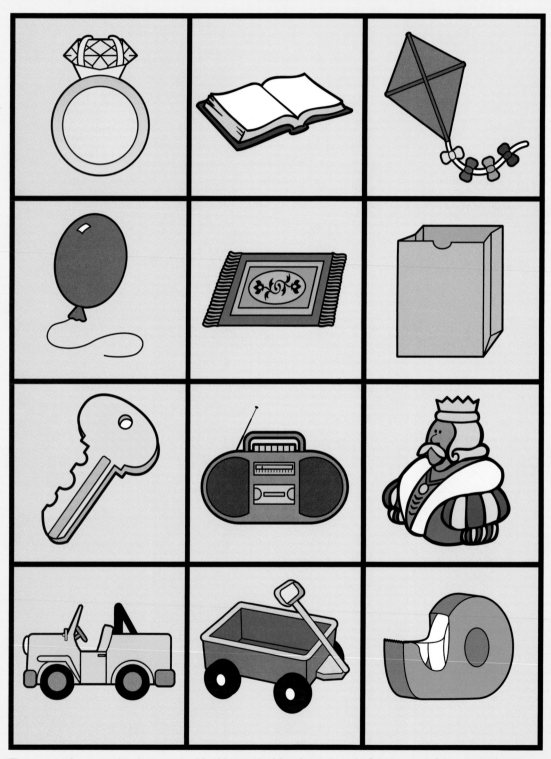

These cards may also be used with "Magnetic Matchups" and "Consonant Concentration" on page 10.

Begins Like Bear

Begins Like Koala

Begins Like Raccoon

Begins Like Bear, Raccoon, or Koala

Cut. Glue.

b bear

r raccoon

k koala

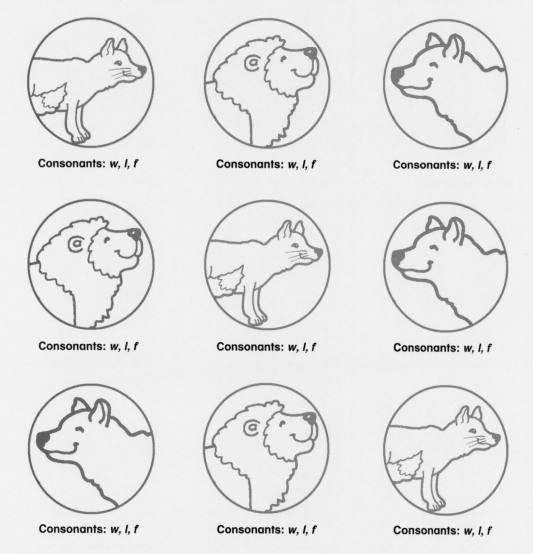

Consonants: *w, l, f*   Consonants: *w, l, f*   Consonants: *w, l, f*

Consonants: *w, l, f*   Consonants: *w, l, f*   Consonants: *w, l, f*

Consonants: *w, l, f*   Consonants: *w, l, f*   Consonants: *w, l, f*

Use these cards with the center mat on page 25.

1. Before using page 25, photocopy page 26 for later use.
2. If desired, laminate the center mat (page 25) and the cards.
3. Cut out the cards.
4. To use, a child turns all the cards full-color side up on a tabletop.
5. The child chooses a picture card and names the picture. She places it beside the picture on the mat that has a matching beginning sound. She continues in this way until each space on the center mat is filled.
6. The child names the pictures in each set, listening to confirm that all the pictures begin with the same sound. She flips each card to check her work.

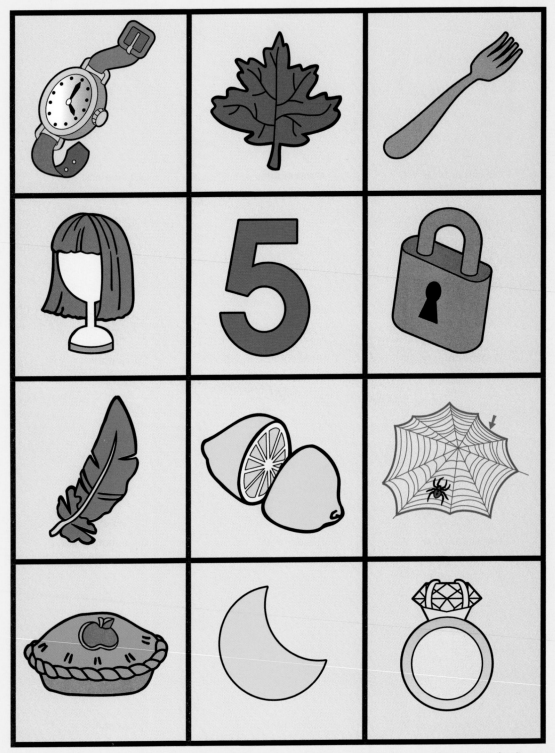

These cards may also be used with "Magnetic Matchups" and "Consonant Concentration" on page 10.

Begins Like Lion

Begins Like Wolf

Begins Like Fox

Begins Like Lion, Wolf, or Fox

Cut. Glue.

Consonants: *h, d, c*

Consonants: *h, d, c*

Consonants: *h, d, c*

Consonants: *h, d, c*

Consonants: *h, d, c*

Consonants: *h, d, c*

Consonants: *h, d, c*

Consonants: *h, d, c*

Consonants: *h, d, c*

Consonants: *h, d, c*

Consonants: *h, d, c*

Consonants: *h, d, c*

Use these cards with the center mat on page 29.

1. Before using page 29, photocopy page 30 for later use.
2. If desired, laminate the center mat (page 29) and the cards.
3. Cut out the cards.
4. To use, a child turns all the cards full-color side up on a tabletop.
5. The child chooses a picture card and names the picture. He places it beside the picture on the mat that has a matching beginning sound. He continues in this way until each space on the center mat is filled.
6. The child names the pictures in each set, listening to confirm that all the pictures begin with the same sound. He flips each card to check his work.

These cards may also be used with "Magnetic Matchups" and "Consonant Concentration" on page 10.

Begins Like Horse

Begins Like Cat

Begins Like Dog

Begins Like Horse, Dog, or Cat

Cut. Glue.

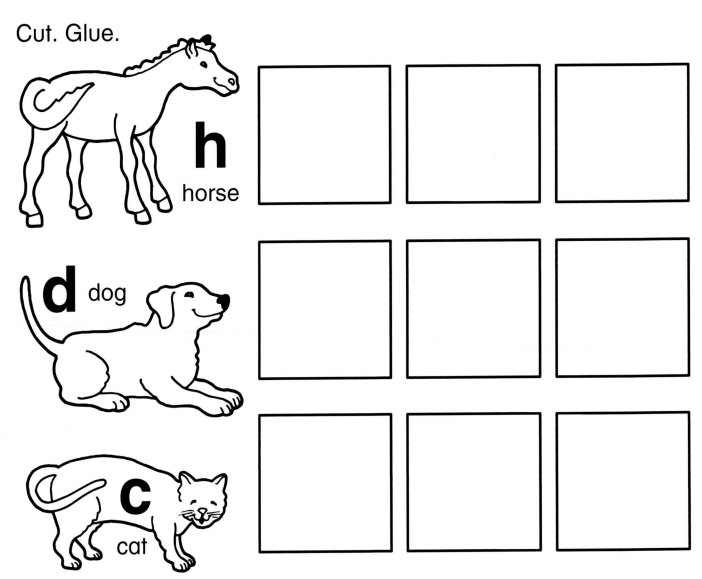

h horse

d dog

c cat

Consonant Digraphs

Contents

Consonant

Time to Ch-Ch-Chant!

Help your youngsters tune in to consonant digraphs with this animal-themed chant. Encourage students to clap to the rhythm of the chant to give it some extra pep!

I'm a chick. My name starts with /ch/.
/Ch/ is the sound. Uh-huh!
I write /ch/ with a *c* and an *h*.
Chick starts with /ch/. Uh-huh!

I'm a sheep. My name starts with /sh/.
/Sh/ is the sound. Uh-huh!
I write /sh/ with an *s* and an *h*.
Sheep starts with /sh/. Uh-huh!

I'm thirteen. My name starts with /th/.
/Th/ is the sound. Uh-huh!
I write /th/ with a *t* and an *h*.
Thirteen starts with /th/. Uh-huh!

I'm a whale. My name starts with /wh/.
/Wh/ is the sound. Uh-huh!
I write /wh/ with a *w* and an *h*.
Whale starts with /wh/. Uh-huh!

Delightful Writing

Use this tactile activity to help youngsters get in touch with the spellings of consonant digraphs. Invite a small group of students to join you at a table. Give each child a walnut-size ball of play dough or clay to flatten into a pancake shape. Say the word *chick* and discuss the two letters that make the /ch/ sound. Have each child use his finger to write *c* and *h* in his dough or clay as you write the letters on a board. Complete the word on the board, pointing out the *c* and the *h* at the beginning. Check each child's work; then have him smooth out the clay before continuing in the same manner with some of the other words shown below.

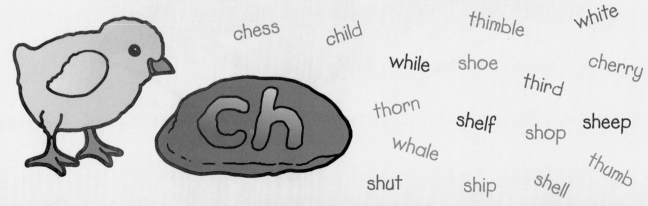

chess   child   thimble   white

while   shoe   cherry

thorn   third

shelf   shop   sheep

whale

shut   ship   shell   thumb

32

Consonants: *h, d, c*

Consonants: *h, d, c*

Consonants: *h, d, c*

Consonants: *h, d, c*

Consonants: *h, d, c*

Consonants: *h, d, c*

Consonants: *h, d, c*

Consonants: *h, d, c*

Consonants: *h, d, c*

Consonants: *h, d, c*

Consonants: *h, d, c*

Consonants: *h, d, c*

Use these cards with the center mat on page 29.

1. Before using page 29, photocopy page 30 for later use.
2. If desired, laminate the center mat (page 29) and the cards.
3. Cut out the cards.
4. To use, a child turns all the cards full-color side up on a tabletop.

5. The child chooses a picture card and names the picture. He places it beside the picture on the mat that has a matching beginning sound. He continues in this way until each space on the center mat is filled.
6. The child names the pictures in each set, listening to confirm that all the pictures begin with the same sound. He flips each card to check his work.

These cards may also be used with "Magnetic Matchups" and "Consonant Concentration" on page 10.

Digraphs

At the Animal Fair

Want to ensure that your phonics lessons are anything but dull? Try this animal fair. To prepare, write the digraphs *sh, ch,* and *wh* on separate index cards, making sure there's one card per child. Begin the game by asking students to stand in a circle. Lay a large plastic hoop on the floor in the center of the circle. Then mix up the digraph cards and give one to each child. Next, tell students that they will pretend to be animals at a funny animal fair. Call out, "Sheep, trot around the ring at the animal fair!" Prompt each child with a *sh* card to hold it up, trot around the hoop, and return to her place in the circle. Continue with two more rounds of the game, calling, "Chicks, hop around the ring!" and "Whales, swim around the ring!" as alternate directions. Before playing additional rounds, have students trade cards. Then call out directions, using the same animals as before but mentioning new movements.

Critter Tongue Twisters

Here's a digraph tongue twister activity that will really help little ones learn to listen! Write the digraphs *ch, sh, th,* and *wh* on separate small squares of paper to make a set of four cards for each child in a small group. Invite youngsters to join you at a table; give each child a set of cards. Then, with a lot of expression, say, "Whales whisper, 'Whoosh!'" Have each child hold up a card to indicate the beginning sound of each word. Next, challenge children to repeat the tongue twister on their own, giving them lots of tries to get it right! Then repeat the activity, using the very silly tongue twisters below!

Cheep!

> Chicks cheep, cheep, cheep.
> Sheep should shower!
> Thirty thick thimbles
> White whales whistle.
> Chimps chase chickens!
> Shy sheep shop.
> Thirsty thistles thump!

Consonant Digraphs

Sounds Different!

Give your youngsters some sound-comparison practice with this easy drawing activity. Visually divide a 12" x 18" sheet of construction paper in half for each child by folding and unfolding the paper. Invite her to draw a seal on the left side of the paper and a sheep on the right. Have the child use large letters to write "s" next to the seal and "sh" next to the sheep. Next, encourage students to discuss the similarities and differences they hear in these beginning sounds. Challenge each child to draw pictures of two more things that begin like *seal* on the left half of the paper and two things that begin like *sheep* on the right half. Help students write matching words to label their pictures if desired. Then listen as each child reads her *s* and then her *sh* words. Later, repeat the activity for *ch* and *c, th* and *t,* and *wh* and *sh.*

Word Workshop

Transparencies are the tools of choice in this word workshop with an auditory slant. To prepare for several consonant digraph workshops, make transparencies of pages 37, 41, 45, and 49. To use the first transparency, designate half of your students to be seals and the other half to be sheep. Project the page 37 transparency onto a screen using an overhead projector. Point to each picture on the transparency, in turn, having students say its name and make its beginning sound. Then encourage each group to take turns suggesting a word that begins with the same sound as its picture. Write suggested words on the transparency, one word per box, until each team has filled its boxes. To increase the challenge, ask for two or three words per box. Review the words listed and help students make observations about the words in each list before ending the activity. On another day, repeat the process to emphasize another digraph by using a transparency from page 41, 45, or 49.

Digraph: *sh*

Digraph: *sh*

Digraph: *sh*

Digraph: *sh*

Digraph: *sh*

Digraph: *sh*

Digraph: *sh*

Digraph: *sh*

Digraph: *sh*

Digraph: *sh*

Digraph: *sh*

Digraph: *sh*

Use these cards with the center mat on page 37.

1. Before using page 37, photocopy page 38 for later use.
2. If desired, laminate the center mat (page 37) and the cards.
3. Cut out the cards.
4. To use, a child turns all the cards full-color side up on a tabletop.

5. The child chooses a picture card and names the picture. She places it near the picture on the mat that has a matching beginning sound. She continues in this way until each space on the center mat is filled.
6. The child names the pictures in each set, listening to confirm that all the pictures begin with the same sound. She flips each card to check her work.

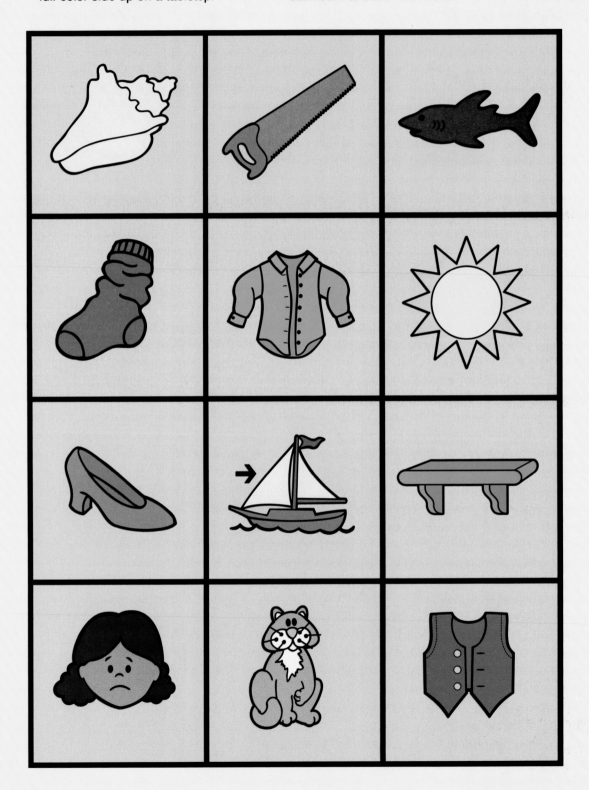

Begins Like Sheep

Begins Like Seal

Begins Like Sheep or Seal

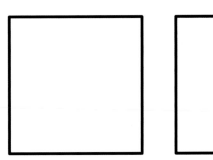

Cut. Glue.

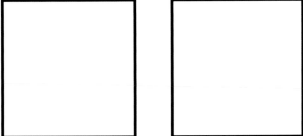

sh
sheep

s
seal

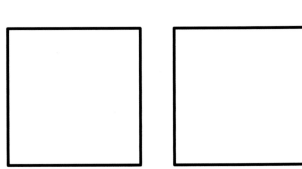

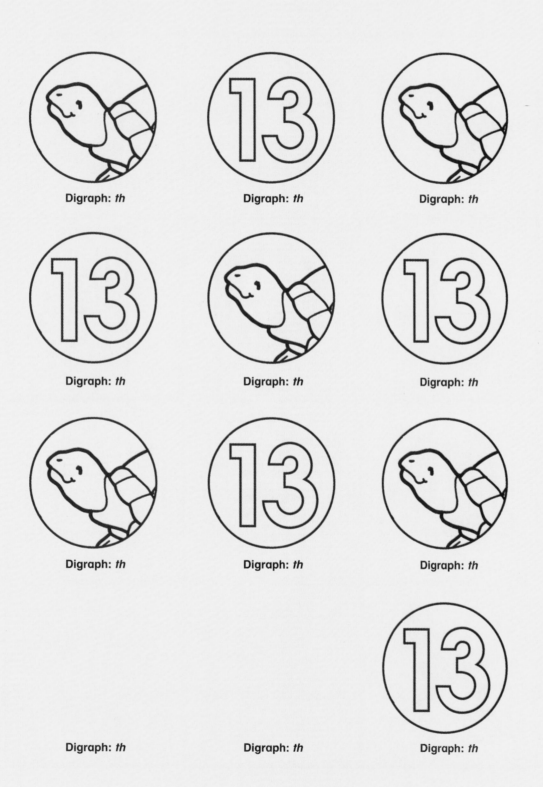

Digraph: *th*

Digraph: *th*

Digraph: *th*

Digraph: *th*

Digraph: *th*

Digraph: *th*

Digraph: *th*

Digraph: *th*

Digraph: *th*

Digraph: *th*

Digraph: *th*

Digraph: *th*

Use these cards with the center mat on page 41.

1. Before using page 41, photocopy page 42 for later use.
2. If desired, laminate the center mat (page 41) and the cards.
3. Cut out the cards.
4. To use, a child turns all the cards full-color side up on a tabletop.

5. The child chooses a picture card and names the picture. He places it near the picture on the mat that has a matching beginning sound. He continues in this way until each space on the center mat is filled.
6. The child names the pictures in each set, listening to confirm that all the pictures begin with the same sound. He flips each card to check his work.

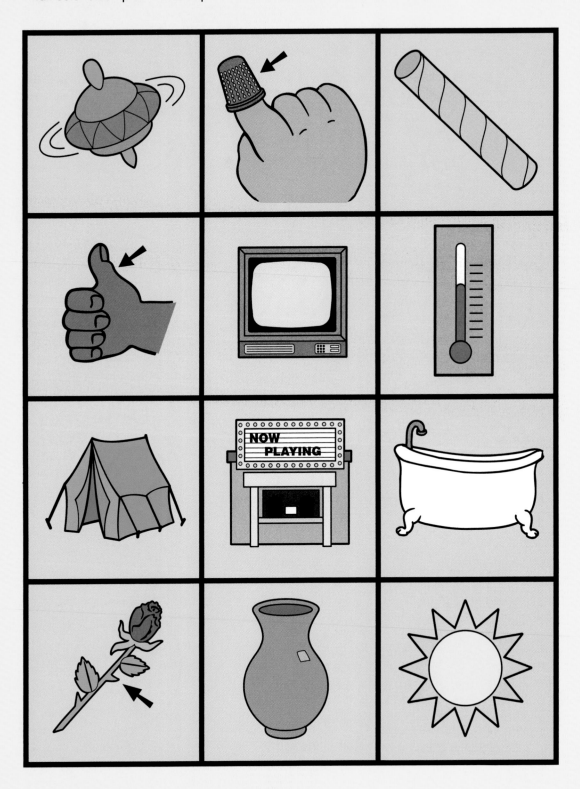

Begins Like Turtle

Begins Like Thirteen

Begins Like Turtle or Thirteen

Cut. Glue.

t
turtle

th
thirteen

13

Digraph: *ch*

Digraph: *ch*

Digraph: *ch*

Digraph: *ch*

Digraph: *ch*

Digraph: *ch*

Digraph: *ch*

Digraph: *ch*

Digraph: *ch*

Digraph: *ch*

Digraph: *ch*

Use these cards with the center mat on page 45.

1. Before using page 45, photocopy page 46 for later use.
2. If desired, laminate the center mat (page 45) and the cards.
3. Cut out the cards.
4. To use, a child turns all the cards full-color side up on a tabletop.
5. The child chooses a picture card and names the picture. She places it near the picture on the mat that has a matching beginning sound. She continues in this way until each space on the center mat is filled.
6. The child names the pictures in each set, listening to confirm that all the pictures begin with the same sound. She flips each card to check her work.

Begins Like Cat

Begins Like Chick

Begins Like Chick or Cat

Cut. Glue.

ch

chick

c

cat

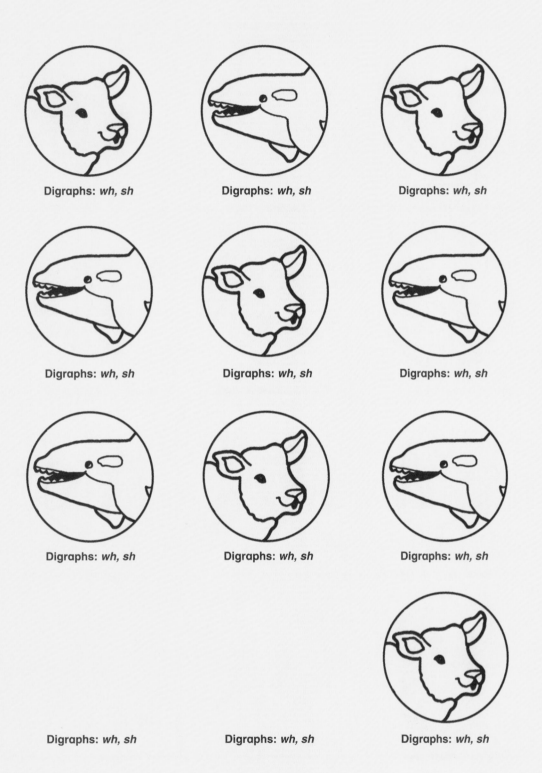

Digraphs: *wh, sh* Digraphs: *wh, sh* Digraphs: *wh, sh*

Digraphs: *wh, sh* Digraphs: *wh, sh* Digraphs: *wh, sh*

Digraphs: *wh, sh* Digraphs: *wh, sh* Digraphs: *wh, sh*

Digraphs: *wh, sh* Digraphs: *wh, sh* Digraphs: *wh, sh*

Use these cards with the center mat on page 49.

1. Before using page 49, photocopy page 50 for later use.
2. If desired, laminate the center mat (page 49) and the cards.
3. Cut out the cards.
4. To use, a child turns all the cards full-color side up on a tabletop.
5. The child chooses a picture card and names the picture. He places it near the animal on the mat that has a matching beginning sound. He continues in this way until each space on the center mat is filled.
6. The child names the pictures in each set, listening to confirm that all the pictures begin with the same sound. He flips each card to check his work.

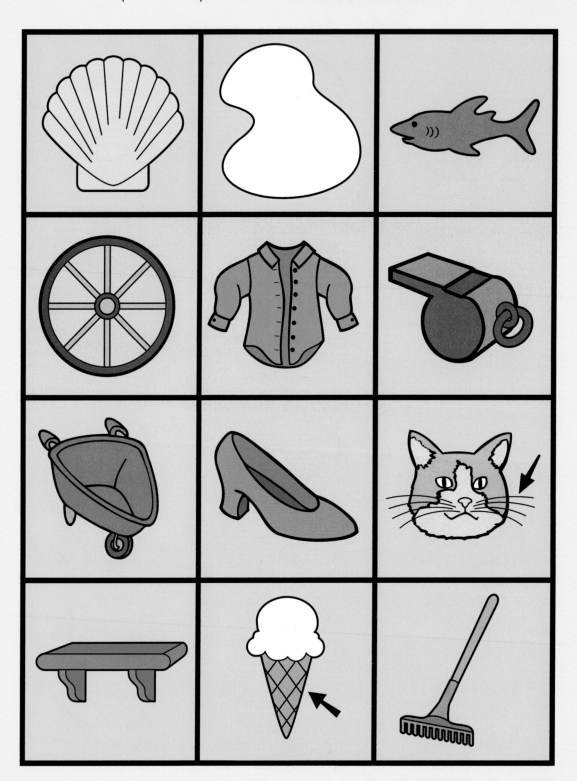

Begins Like Whale

Begins Like Sheep

Begins Like Sheep or Whale

Cut. Glue.

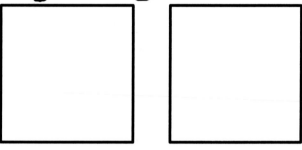
sh
sheep

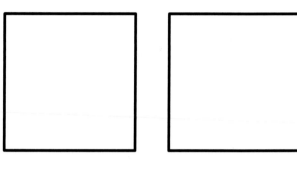
wh
whale

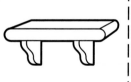

Consonant Blends

Contents

Consonant

Bouncy Blends Chant

Blend rhythm and rhyme with learning in this oral language activity. For each animal that you feature, draw a simple sketch of it on the board and label it with its name and its name's initial blend. As you feature a different animal in the chant below, point out the blend, the word, and the picture on the board. Invite your youngsters to clap to the rhythm of the chant to give it a bit of bounce!

Blend a(n) [c] and a(n) [r] to make a new sound.
What is the special sound you get?
Blend [/k/] and [/r/] to make the sound.
It's the beginning of [crab]; you bet!

Repeat the verse, making the appropriate substitutions for frog, skunk, snake, stork, and swan.

Blend a(n) [b] and a(n) [l] to make a new sound.
What is the special sound you get?
Blend [/b/] and [/l/] to make the sound.
It's the beginning of [blue jay]; you bet!

Repeat the verse, making the appropriate substitutions for clown fish, dragon, flamingo, and spider.

Writing Blends

Help your young animal lovers review consonant blends with this easy animal-themed activity. Give each child an individual whiteboard or chalkboard and something to write with. Say the name of an animal mentioned below, prompting students to make the beginning sound of the name. As each child makes the sound, have her write the matching letters. Check each child's work; then ask students to name other words that begin with the same consonant blend. Before moving on to name another animal, have children erase their boards.

swan	clown fish
skunk	blue jay
spider	crab
snake	frog
stork	dragon
flamingo	

Blends

The Merry-Go-Round

Invite students to mimic animals on a merry-go-round with this silly song activity. To prepare, write the blends *sk*, *sp*, and *sw* on separate index cards, making sure there's one card per child. Begin the game by asking students to stand in a circle to represent a merry-go-round; explain that carousels often feature other animals in addition to horses. Shuffle the index cards and give one to each child. Sing the song, prompting students with cards representing the beginning blend in *skunk* to skip around the outside of the circle as they pretend to be—not carousel horses—but carousel skunks! After the last line of the song, have children return to their original places in the circle. Continue with two more rounds of the song, substituting swans and spiders for skunks. Then have students trade cards and play the game again! Later, repeat the game using different blend cards and animals.

*(sung to the tune of
"He's Got the Whole World in His Hands")*

Let's watch the [skunks] on the merry-go-round.
Let's watch the [skunks] going up and down.
Let's watch the [skunks] on the merry-go-round.
Let's watch the [skunks] go round and round!

Our Big Blends Book

Big Blends Book

Little learners will get lots of practice using consonant blends as they make and read a cooperative book. Make copies of the 11 blend miniposters on pages 156–159 so that each of your children will have one. Have each child choose a miniposter to color and glue to a large sheet of white construction paper. Ask each child to think about that animal word and other words that start with the blend. Give him several days to locate (or draw) and label pictures of other things that begin with the featured blend. When all the pages are complete, bind them between construction paper covers. Write the title "Our Big Blends Book" on the cover, read the book to your class, and put it in your book corner for independent student reading.

Consonant Blends

Blends Concentration Game

If you're looking for a game that gets your students focused on blends, you've come to the right place. Cut out 11 two-inch squares of construction paper. Use a marker to label each one with a different blend: *sw, sk, st, sn, sp, fl, cl, bl, dr, cr, fr*. Make construction paper copies of the picture cards on pages 56, 60, 64, and 68. Cut out one picture card for each blend; then place those 11 selected cards and the blend cards in a zippered plastic bag for storage. (If desired, use the remaining picture cards and additional blend cards to make several sets of Concentration games for independent student use or for practice at home.)

To play with a small group of children, place all 22 cards facedown on a tabletop. Have children take turns flipping two cards per turn in search of a blend-picture match. Children who find matches hold on to those cards as play continues. When all the matches have been located, everyone's a winner!

sk

Transparently Blended

What do you get when you use your overhead projector with transparencies of the center mats in this book? Some great conversation about blends—that's what! To prepare for four consonant blend discussions, make transparencies of pages 57, 61, 65, and 69. For the first discussion, project the transparency of page 57 onto a screen. Point to each picture on the transparency, in turn, having students say its name and make the beginning blend sounds. Divide your youngsters into three groups. Assign one group to be skunks, one to be spiders, and the third to be swans! Then encourage each team to take turns suggesting a word that begins with the same blend as its animal's name. Write suggested words on the transparency, three or four per box, until each team has filled its boxes. Review the words listed and help students make observations about the words in each list before ending the activity. Erase the words and repeat the activity, assigning a different animal to each group. On another day, repeat the process to emphasize other blends using a transparency of page 61, 65, or 69.

Blends: *sp, sw, sk*

Blends: *sp, sw, sk*

Blends: *sp, sw, sk*

Blends: *sp, sw, sk*

Blends: *sp, sw, sk*

Blends: *sp, sw, sk*

Blends: *sp, sw, sk*

Blends: *sp, sw, sk*

Blends: *sp, sw, sk*

Blends: *sp, sw, sk*   Blends: *sp, sw, sk*   Blends: *sp, sw, sk*

Use these cards with the center mat on page 57.

1. Before using page 57, photocopy page 58 for later use.
2. If desired, laminate the center mat (page 57) and the cards.
3. Cut out the cards.
4. To use, a child turns all the cards full-color side up on a tabletop.
5. The child chooses a picture card and names the picture. She places it beside the picture on the mat that has matching beginning sounds. She continues in this way until each space on the center mat is filled.
6. The child names the pictures in each set, listening to confirm that all the pictures begin with the same sounds. She flips each card to check her work.

These cards may also be used with "Blends Concentration Game" on page 54.

Begins Like Swan

Begins Like Spider

Begins Like Skunk

Begins Like Swan, Skunk, or Spider

Cut. Glue.

 **sw**
swan

 **sk**
skunk

 **sp**
spider

©The Mailbox® • *Sounds Like Fun: Phenomenal Phonics* • TEC60914

Blends: *sn, st, sp*

Blends: *sn, st, sp*

Blends: *sn, st, sp*

Blends: *sn, st, sp*

Blends: *sn, st, sp*

Blends: *sn, st, sp*

Blends: *sn, st, sp*

Blends: *sn, st, sp*

Blends: *sn, st, sp*

Blends: *sn, st, sp*

Blends: *sn, st, sp*

Blends: *sn, st, sp*

Use these cards with the center mat on page 61.

1. Before using page 61, photocopy page 62 for later use.
2. If desired, laminate the center mat (page 61) and the cards.
3. Cut out the cards.
4. To use, a child turns all the cards full-color side up on a tabletop.
5. The child chooses a picture card and names the picture. He places it beside the picture on the mat that has matching beginning sounds. He continues in this way until each space on the center mat is filled.
6. The child names the pictures in each set, listening to confirm that all the pictures begin with the same sounds. He flips each card to check his work.

These cards may also be used with "Blends Concentration Game" on page 54.

©The Mailbox® • *Sounds Like Fun: Phenomenal Phonics* • TEC60914

Begins Like Stork

Begins Like Snake

Begins Like Spider

Begins Like Stork, Snake, or Spider

Cut. Glue.

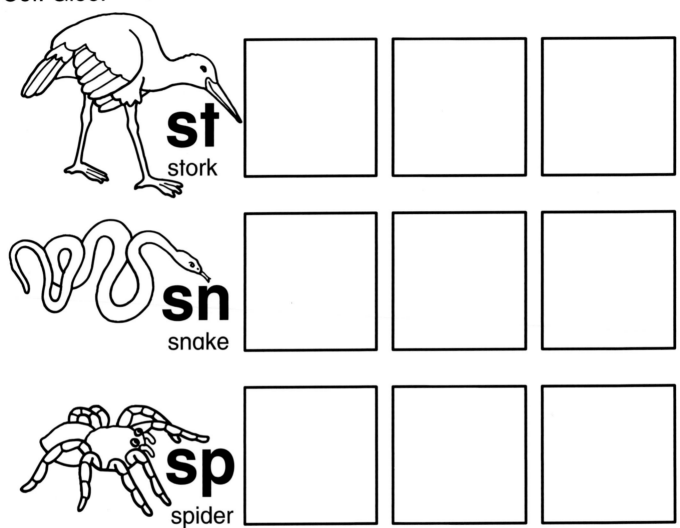

st stork

sn snake

sp spider

Blends: *cl, fl, bl*

Blends: *cl, fl, bl*

Blends: *cl, fl, bl*

Blends: *cl, fl, bl*

Blends: *cl, fl, bl*

Blends: *cl, fl, bl*

Blends: *cl, fl, bl*

Blends: *cl, fl, bl*

Blends: *cl, fl, bl*

Blends: *cl, fl, bl*   Blends: *cl, fl, bl*   Blends: *cl, fl, bl*

Use these cards with the center mat on page 65.

1. Before using page 65, photocopy page 66 for later use.
2. If desired, laminate the center mat (page 65) and the cards.
3. Cut out the cards.
4. To use, a child turns all the cards full-color side up on a tabletop.
5. The child chooses a picture card and names the picture. She places it beside the picture on the mat that has matching beginning sounds. She continues in this way until each space on the center mat is filled.
6. The child names the pictures in each set, listening to confirm that all the pictures begin with the same sounds. She flips each card to check her work.

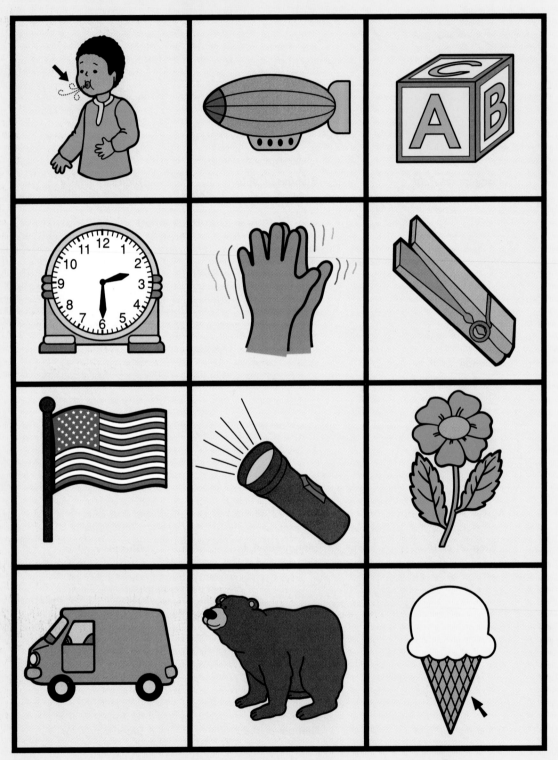

These cards may also be used with "Blends Concentration Game" on page 54.

Begins Like Flamingo

Begins Like Clown Fish

Begins Like Blue Jay

Begins Like Flamingo, Clown Fish, or Blue Jay

Cut. Glue.

 **fl**
flamingo

 **cl**
clown fish

 **bl**
blue jay

Blends: *cr, dr, fr*   Blends: *cr, dr, fr*   Blends: *cr, dr, fr*

Blends: *cr, dr, fr*   Blends: *cr, dr, fr*   Blends: *cr, dr, fr*

Blends: *cr, dr, fr*   Blends: *cr, dr, fr*   Blends: *cr, dr, fr*

Blends: *cr, dr, fr*   Blends: *cr, dr, fr*   Blends: *cr, dr, fr*

Use these cards with the center mat on page 69.

1. Before using page 69, photocopy page 70 for later use.
2. If desired, laminate the center mat (page 69) and the cards.
3. Cut out the cards.
4. To use, a child turns all the cards full-color side up on a tabletop.
5. The child chooses a picture card and names the picture. He places it beside the picture on the mat that has matching beginning sounds. He continues in this way until each space on the center mat is filled.
6. The child names the pictures in each set, listening to confirm that all the pictures begin with the same sounds. He flips each card to check his work.

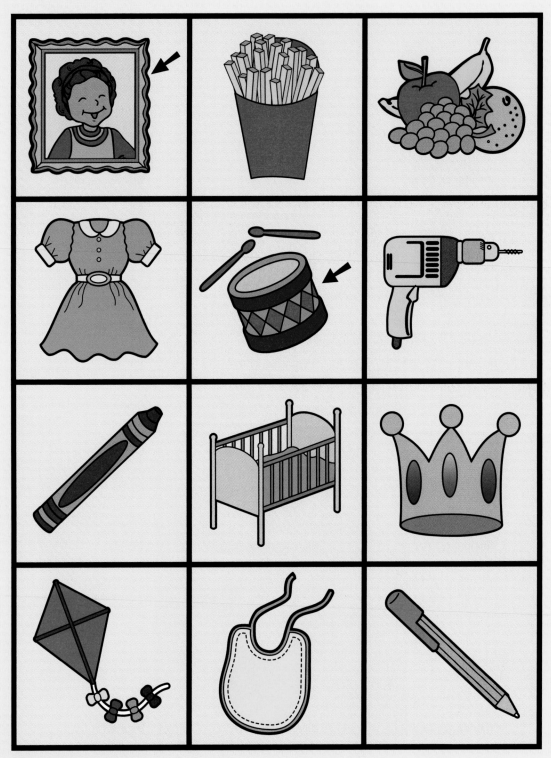

These cards may also be used with "Blends Concentration Game" on page 54.

Begins Like Dragon

Begins Like Crab

Begins Like Frog

Begins Like Dragon, Crab, or Frog

Cut. Glue.

©The Mailbox® • *Sounds Like Fun: Phenomenal Phonics* • TEC60914

Word Families

Contents

Juggling Word Families

Turn word family conversations into festive fun with this perky tune and a circus juggling routine. To begin, write the words *cat, ram,* and *crab* on the board. Above each word, write the corresponding word ending *(at, am,* or *ab)* and surround it with circles to represent juggling balls. Before singing, talk about each animal name and its word ending. After a verse is sung, have children name two words that belong in the corresponding word family. As children identify these words, write each word in a different circle. Continue singing and writing until each circle is filled. Then have children read the words in each word family as they listen for the identical endings.

(sung to the tune of "Take Me Out to the Ballgame")

Let's go down to the circus.
Silly critters are there.
There is a [cat] that can juggle. Hey!
That [cat] juggles and juggles all day!
Only [at] words are what she juggles!
[Cat] thinks she is the best.
Juggle [at], [at], [at], and [at],
And leave out the rest!
Repeat the song, making the appropriate substitutions for ram *and* crab.

Poster Poses

As children craft these silly posters, word families are certainly in the limelight. To prepare the activity for a group of four students, write each sentence below on a separate sentence strip. Read the sentences with students and talk about the words on each strip that are from the same word family. Invite each child to choose one sentence to illustrate on art paper. Provide reading and brainstorming support as needed. Have children who are ready for a bigger challenge include more than two juggled items from the corresponding word family. When the illustrations are complete, have children label each poster with at least three words from the featured word family and share their posters with their classmates. Step right up! See the world's most talented dog juggling a log and a frog!

The cat juggles a hat and a mat.
The dog juggles a log and a frog.
The pig juggles a wig and a fig.
The hen juggles a pen and a ten.

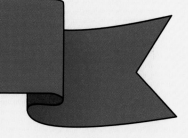

Families

How Big Is This Family?

Here's an easy collaborative activity to motivate your youngsters to think of many words that belong in word families. On the back of a thin paper plate, have a child draw a cat and label it. Meanwhile, have four other children similarly prepare plates featuring *dog, pig, crab,* and *hen.* On each plate, cut a two-inch slit where the plate bottom and the rim meet. Review *cat* and its word family with students. Then, for each word family, challenge a small group of youngsters to brainstorm words that belong to that word family. Have each group member write a selected word repeatedly on a 1" x 9" strip of construction paper. After all the groups' words have been recorded on strips, have each group make its strips into a paper chain. Help students loop the last link through their group's paper plate. Display each of the chains and have students read the words in each word family. Talk about which word families have more or fewer words. Encourage students to be on the lookout for other words that could be added to the word family chains.

In the Center Ring

Put word families in the spotlight with this kid-pleasing activity. To prepare for the activity, write each of the following on separate index cards: *am, at, en, ig, og,* and *ub.* Divide your children into six groups and give each group one of the word family cards. Have each child in the group program a card with a different word of his choice from the word family. Encourage collaboration. Verify that each child's card matches his word family before beginning the game by asking students to stand in a circle. Next, hold up the *am* card and say, "All *am* family performers, go to the center ring!" Prompt each child with an *am* card to hold it up, move to the center of the circle, and strike a silly pose. Then, with a flourish, signal for each of these students, in turn, to ceremoniously read his card before returning to his original place in the circle. Continue with five more rounds of the game: one round for each word family represented by the letter cards. To play additional rounds of the game, have students trade cards.

Word Families

Word-Sorting Center

This center idea gives children an opportunity to independently sort three sets of word family cards. In the top row of a pocket chart, display three different student-made animal picture cards: dog, hen, and ram. Place the pocket chart in a center along with a key and word cards featuring the words below. To use the center, invite a child to sort the word cards by family and then display the cards in the chart under the appropriate animal picture. As he uses the key to verify that each card is in the right place, have him remove the card from the pocket chart.

men	fog	ham
ten	hog	jam
pen	log	yam
Ben	frog	slam

A Workshop of Words

Challenge students to generate and compare words with this word family activity. Make transparencies of the center mats on pages 77, 81, 85, 89, 93, and 97 to create six word-generating games. To use the transparency from page 77, divide your youngsters into two groups. Assign one group the *at* family and the other the *an* family. Project the transparency onto a screen. Point to each picture, in turn, and have students say its name and identify the word family. Have the teams take turns suggesting words that belong in their word families. Write suggested words on the transparency, one word per box. After writing each word, allow a team representative to roll a die. If the die lands on six, the team gets an extra turn. When one team wins by filling its boxes with words, allow the other team to suggest words to complete its boxes. Then encourage students to compare the two word families, discussing how they are alike and how they are different. Erase the words and repeat the activity, assigning a different word family to each group. Use the remaining transparencies in the same manner.

Word Families: *at, an*

Word Families: *at, an*

Word Families: *at, an*

Word Families: *at, an*

Word Families: *at, an*

Word Families: *at, an*

Word Families: *at, an*

Word Families: *at, an*

Word Families: *at, an*

Word Families: *at, an*

Word Families: *at, an*

Word Families: *at, an*

Use these cards with the center mat on page 77.

1. Before using page 77, photocopy page 78 for later use.
2. If desired, laminate the center mat (page 77) and the cards.
3. Cut out the cards.
4. To use, a child turns all the cards green side up on a tabletop.
5. The child chooses a picture card and names the picture. He places it beneath the picture on the mat that ends the same. He continues in this way until each picture is placed. Using his letter-sound knowledge, he matches a word card to each picture.
6. The child names the pictures and reads the words in each set, listening to confirm that all of the pictures and words end the same. He flips each card to check his work.

hat	rat	mat
van	fan	man

©The Mailbox® • *Sounds Like Fun: Phenomenal Phonics* • TEC60914

an

at

Ends Like
Cat
or
Can

Ends Like Cat or Can

Cut. Glue the pictures to match.
Then glue the words to match the pictures.

cat

at

can

an

©The Mailbox® • *Sounds Like Fun: Phenomenal Phonics* • TEC60914

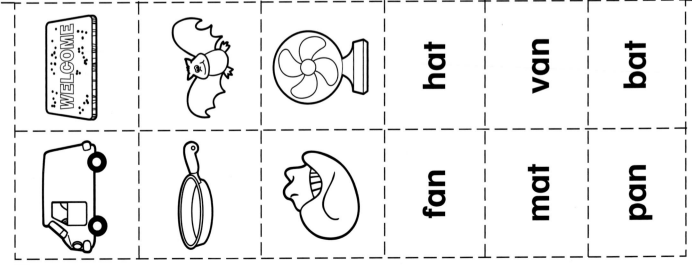

hat   van   bat

fan   mat   pan

Word Families: *am, ag* Word Families: *am, ag* Word Families: *am, ag*

Word Families: *am, ag* Word Families: *am, ag* Word Families: *am, ag*

Word Families: *am, ag* Word Families: *am, ag* Word Families: *am, ag*

Word Families: *am, ag* Word Families: *am, ag* Word Families: *am, ag*

Use these cards with the center mat on page 81.

1. Before using page 81, photocopy page 82 for later use.
2. If desired, laminate the center mat (page 81) and the cards.
3. Cut out the cards.
4. To use, a child turns all the cards green side up on a tabletop.

5. The child chooses a picture card and names the picture. She places it beneath the picture on the mat that ends the same. She continues in this way until each picture is placed. Using her letter-sound knowledge, she matches a word card to each picture.
6. The child names the pictures and reads the words in each set, listening to confirm that all of the pictures and words end the same. She flips each card to check her work.

ham	**yam**	**jam**
tag	**wag**	**flag**

©The Mailbox® • *Sounds Like Fun: Phenomenal Phonics* • TEC60914

ag

am

Ends Like
Ram
or
Bag

©The Mailbox® • Sounds Like Fun: Phenomenal Phonics • TEC60914

Ends Like Ram or Bag

Cut. Glue the pictures to match.
Then glue the words to match the pictures.

ram   **am**   bag   **ag**

ham tag yam

flag jam wag

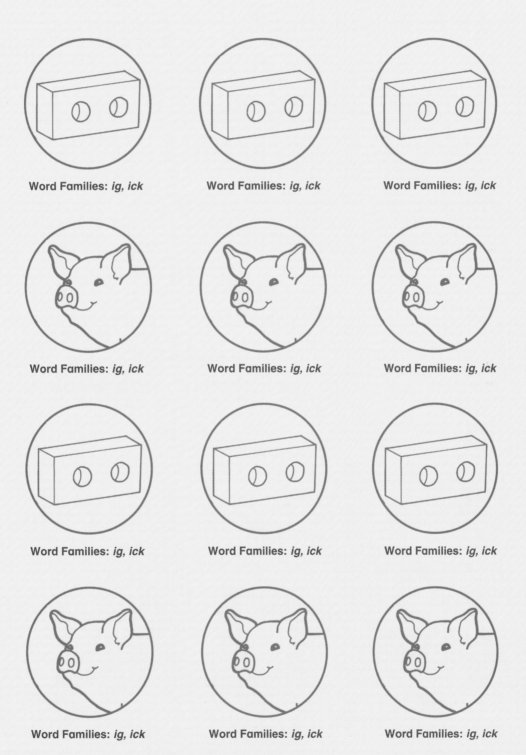

Word Families: *ig, ick*   Word Families: *ig, ick*   Word Families: *ig, ick*

Word Families: *ig, ick*   Word Families: *ig, ick*   Word Families: *ig, ick*

Word Families: *ig, ick*   Word Families: *ig, ick*   Word Families: *ig, ick*

Word Families: *ig, ick*   Word Families: *ig, ick*   Word Families: *ig, ick*

Use these cards with the center mat on page 85.

1. Before using page 85, photocopy page 86 for later use.
2. If desired, laminate the center mat (page 85) and the cards.
3. Cut out the cards.
4. To use, a child turns all the cards green side up on a tabletop.

5. The child chooses a picture card and names the picture. He places it beneath the picture on the mat that ends the same. He continues in this way until each picture is placed. Using his letter-sound knowledge, he matches a word card to each picture.
6. The child names the pictures and reads the words in each set, listening to confirm that all of the pictures and words end the same. He flips each card to check his work.

kick	**chick**	**stick**
pig	**wig**	**dig**

ick

ig

Ends Like
Pig
or
Brick

Ends Like Pig or Brick

Cut. Glue the pictures to match.
Then glue the words to match the pictures.

pig   **ig**   brick   **ick**

©The Mailbox® • *Sounds Like Fun: Phenomenal Phonics* • TEC60914

wig   chick   pig

kick   dig   stick

Word Families: *op, og*

Word Families: *op, og*

Word Families: *op, og*

Word Families: *op, og*

Word Families: *op, og*

Word Families: *op, og*

Word Families: *op, og*

Word Families: *op, og*

Word Families: *op, og*

Word Families: *op, og*

Word Families: *op, og*

Word Families: *op, og*

Use these cards with the center mat on page 89.

1. Before using page 89, photocopy page 90 for later use.
2. If desired, laminate the center mat (page 89) and the cards.
3. Cut out the cards.
4. To use, a child turns all the cards green side up on a tabletop.

5. The child chooses a picture card and names the picture. She places it beneath the picture on the mat that ends the same. She continues in this way until each picture is placed. Using her letter-sound knowledge, she matches a word card to each picture.
6. The child names the pictures and reads the words in each set, listening to confirm that all of the pictures and words end the same. She flips each card to check her work.

hop	drop	top
log	smog	frog

©The Mailbox® • *Sounds Like Fun: Phenomenal Phonics* • TEC60914

op

og

Ends Like
Dog
or
Mop

Ends Like Dog or Mop

Cut. Glue the pictures to match.
Then glue the words to match the pictures.

og dog

op mop

©The Mailbox® • *Sounds Like Fun: Phenomenal Phonics* • TEC60914

top

log

hop

frog

stop

smog

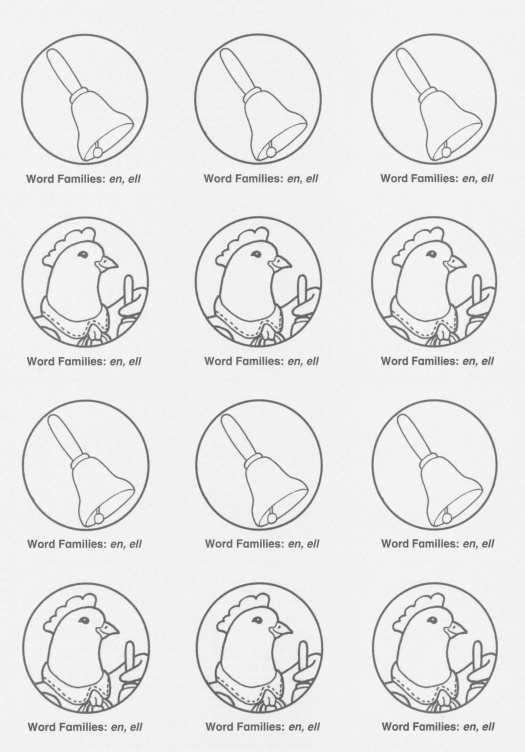

Word Families: *en, ell*   Word Families: *en, ell*   Word Families: *en, ell*

Word Families: *en, ell*   Word Families: *en, ell*   Word Families: *en, ell*

Word Families: *en, ell*   Word Families: *en, ell*   Word Families: *en, ell*

Word Families: *en, ell*   Word Families: *en, ell*   Word Families: *en, ell*

Use these cards with the center mat on page 93.

1. Before using page 93, photocopy page 94 for later use.
2. If desired, laminate the center mat (page 93) and the cards.
3. Cut out the cards.
4. To use, a child turns all the cards green side up on a tabletop.

5. The child chooses a picture card and names the picture. He places it beneath the picture on the mat that ends the same. He continues in this way until each picture is placed. Using his letter-sound knowledge, he matches a word card to each picture.
6. The child names the pictures and reads the words in each set, listening to confirm that all of the pictures and words end the same. He flips each card to check his work.

| shell | well | yell |
| men | ten | pen |

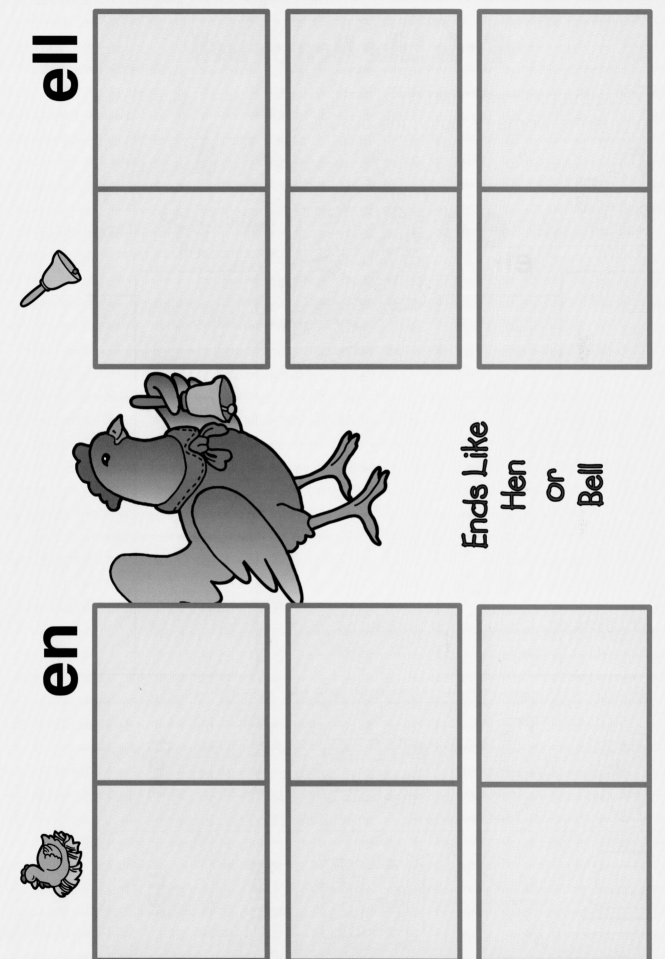

ell

en

Ends Like
Hen
or
Bell

Ends Like Hen or Bell

Cut. Glue the pictures to match.
Then glue the words to match the pictures.

hen

en

bell

ell

©The Mailbox® • *Sounds Like Fun: Phenomenal Phonics* • TEC60914

pen

well

men

shell

ten

yell

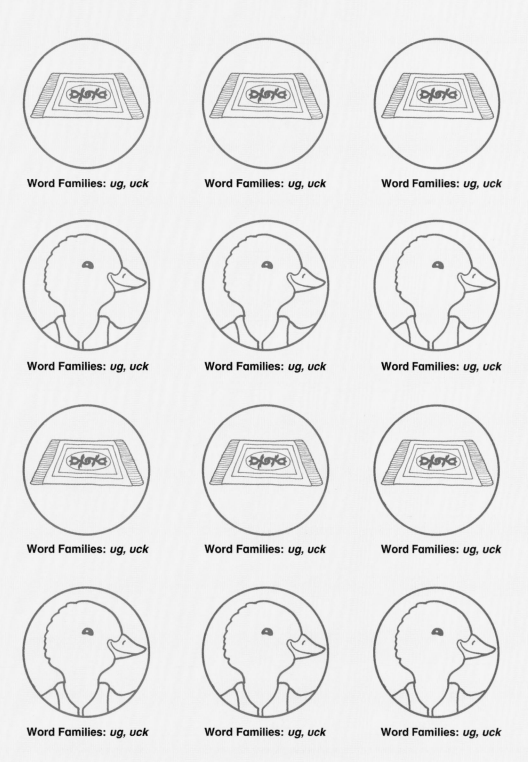

Word Families: *ug, uck*

Word Families: *ug, uck*

Word Families: *ug, uck*

Word Families: *ug, uck*

Word Families: *ug, uck*

Word Families: *ug, uck*

Word Families: *ug, uck*

Word Families: *ug, uck*

Word Families: *ug, uck*

Word Families: *ug, uck*

Word Families: *ug, uck*

Word Families: *ug, uck*

Use these cards with the center mat on page 97.

1. Before using page 97, photocopy page 98 for later use.
2. If desired, laminate the center mat (page 97) and the cards.
3. Cut out the cards.
4. To use, a child turns all the cards green side up on a tabletop.

5. The child chooses a picture card and names the picture. She places it beneath the picture on the mat that ends the same. She continues in this way until each picture is placed. Using her letter-sound knowledge, she matches a word card to each picture.
6. The child names the pictures and reads the words in each set, listening to confirm that all of the pictures and words end the same. She flips each card to check her work.

mug	jug	plug
puck	**stuck**	**truck**

ug

uck

Ends Like
Duck
or
Rug

©The Mailbox® • Sounds Like Fun: Phenomenal Phonics • TEC60914

Ends Like Duck or Rug

Cut. Glue the pictures to match.
Then glue the words to match the pictures.

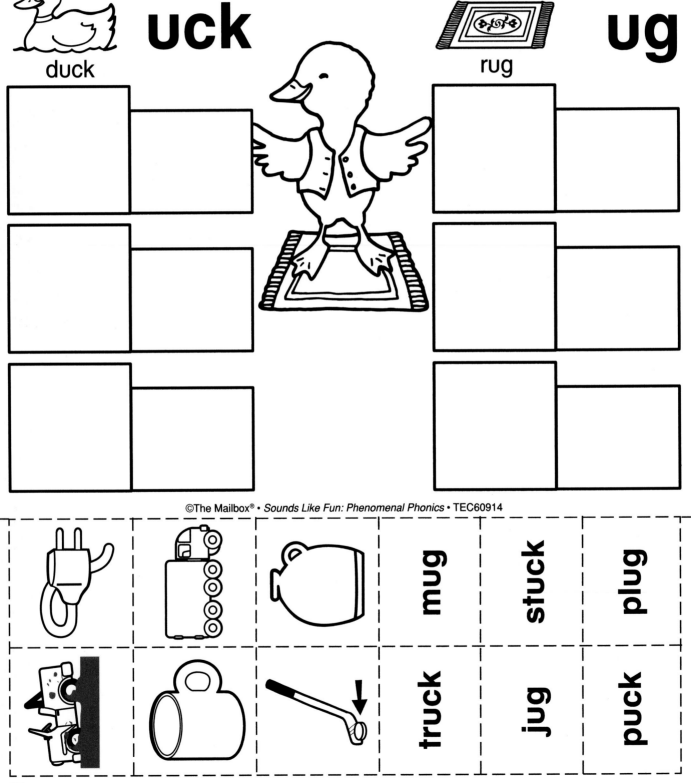

uck

duck

ug

rug

©The Mailbox® • *Sounds Like Fun: Phenomenal Phonics* • TEC60914

mug

stuck

plug

truck

jug

puck

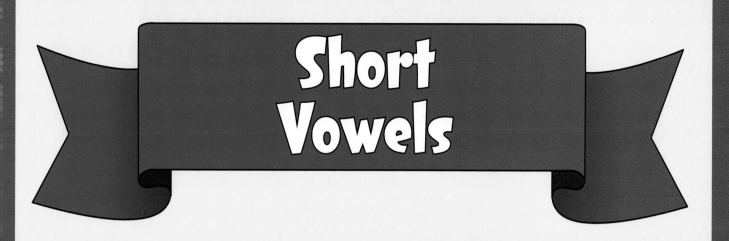

Short Vowels

Contents

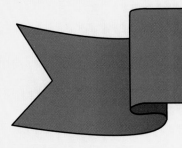

Short

Zoo Critters

Sing this little tune to introduce your children to some animal names that begin with short-vowel sounds.

(sung to the tune of "Baa, Baa, Black Sheep")

Of the critters in the zoo,
I like [antelopes] best; don't you?
[Antelope] starts with *[a],* it's true:
[/A/, /a/, antelope] in the zoo.
Of the critters in the zoo,
I like [antelopes] best; don't you?

Repeat the verse, making the appropriate substitutions for elephant, iguana, *and* otter.

A Special Touch

Help your youngsters review letter-sound relationships with this small-group activity. Write the letters *a, e, i, o,* and *u* on several corrugated paper strips (such as previously used bulletin board borders). Place the strips on a table and invite a small group of youngsters to join you there. Say, in turn, the name of each animal from this section (antelope, elephant, iguana, otter, and umbrella cockatoo); prompt students to repeat the beginning sound of each name and to use their fingers to trace the corresponding letter on the strips. Continue in this manner, supplying other words that begin with short-vowel sounds. Then say, in turn, several consonant-vowel-consonant words (*mat, pot,* and *him,* for example) and have children listen for and trace the vowel that makes the medial sound.

Vowels

Zookeeper Says

Here's a phonics game your children don't have to sit still for! Make a supply of vowel cards or die-cut vowels so that a similar number of children will receive each vowel. Begin the game by asking students to stand in a line in a large open space. Mix up the letters and give one to each child; then stand facing the students. Next, explain that you'll be the zookeeper and will ask that different animals perform different actions. Then call out a direction such as, "Zookeeper says, 'Antelopes, trot forward!'" Prompt students holding the letter that is heard at the beginning of *antelopes* to come forward, make the short *a* sound, and then return to their original places. Continue with more rounds of the game, varying the animal and the movement and periodically having children exchange letters so that each player gets in on varied action! Animals to include are alligators, ants, elephants, iguanas, ostriches, otters, oxen, and umbrella cockatoos.

Pocket Pals

This pocket chart activity gets students busy writing words that contain short-vowel sounds. Divide youngsters into five groups and assign each group a vowel and a key word *(a* and *antelope, e* and *elephant, i* and *iguana, o* and *otter,* and *u* and *umbrella cockatoo).* Ask each group to have a representative draw the animal on a blank pocket chart card and label it with the letter. Then have the students of each group think of other words that include the same vowel sound as the sound at the beginning of their key word. (The vowel may be at the beginning or in the middle of the words they're writing.) Provide assistance, if needed, as children write each word on a separate card. Have groups put their picture-word cards at the top of a pocket chart as column headers and then add their word cards beneath them. Ask each group to read its words to the class and to explain how the words relate to the picture word.

Short Vowels

Perfect Pairings

Get the wiggles out while working on phonics skills. Label each of the four corners and the center of your classroom with a different vowel. Also prepare for this game by cutting out photocopies of the pictures at the bottoms of pages 106, 110, 114, and 118. Eliminate the ones that feature words with initial consonants and then place the remaining pictures in a gift bag.

To play the game, ask each student to pull a picture from the bag. Then have each child walk around holding his picture in front of him as he searches for someone who holds a picture whose name begins with the same short-vowel sound (but is not the same word). When he locates a partner and they agree that their beginning sounds match, have them move to the part of the room labeled to match their sound. Once there, the group of children confirms that all its pictures' names begin the same. If necessary, help stragglers find their groups. Discuss the groupings, answer any questions, and have children put their squares back in the bag to begin the next round.

Medial Vowel Relay

For practice with short vowels in the middle position, scatter on a tabletop the picture and word rectangles from three copies each of pages 78, 82, 86, 90, 94, and 98. Divide your children into four teams and have them line up several feet away from the table for a relay. Call out a key word with a medial short vowel (such as *hop* or *bit*). Give each team a moment to confer about the middle sound; then start the relay by having the first child on each team run to the table, locate a word or picture whose name has the same medial short vowel as the key word, and bring it back to his team. After each child has had a turn, have the team members look over their collection to confirm that all their words or pictures feature the same middle short-vowel sound as the key word did. Teams who meet that goal score one point for the round. Children then return their rectangles to the table and listen for the key word for the next round.

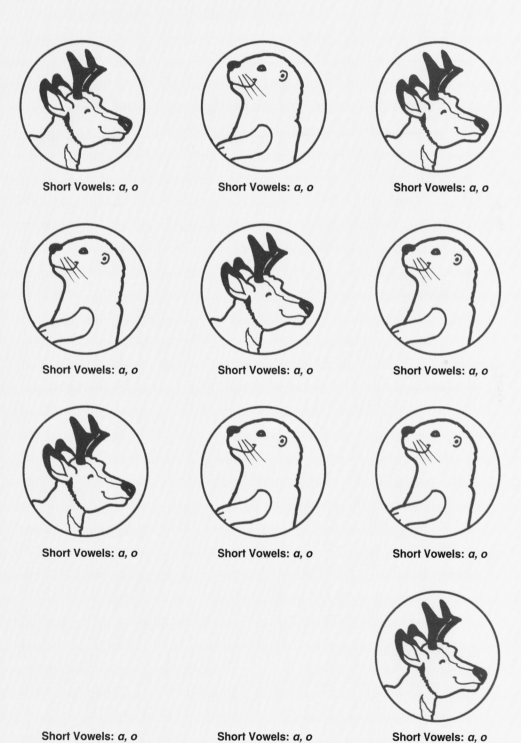

Short Vowels: *a, o*

Short Vowels: *a, o*

Short Vowels: *a, o*

Short Vowels: *a, o*

Short Vowels: *a, o*

Short Vowels: *a, o*

Short Vowels: *a, o*

Short Vowels: *a, o*

Short Vowels: *a, o*

Short Vowels: *a, o*

Short Vowels: *a, o*

Short Vowels: *a, o*

Use these cards with the center mat on page 105.

1. Before using page 105, photocopy page 106 for later use.
2. If desired, laminate the center mat (page 105) and the cards.
3. Cut out the cards.
4. To use, a child turns all the cards full-color side up on a tabletop.
5. The child chooses a picture card and names the picture. He places it near the picture on the mat that has a matching beginning sound. He continues in this way until each space on the center mat is filled.
6. The child names the pictures in each set, listening to confirm that all the pictures begin with the same sound. He flips each card to check his work.

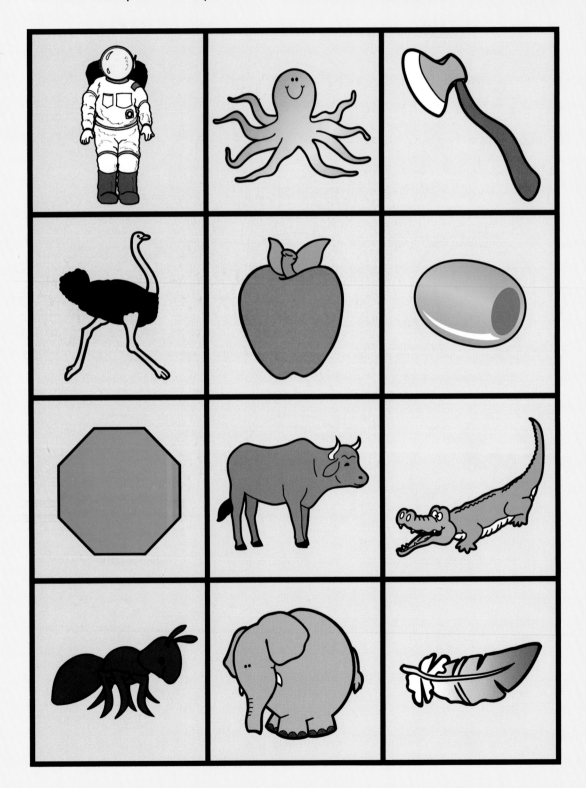

Begins Like Otter

Begins Like Antelope

Begins Like Otter or Antelope

Cut. Glue.

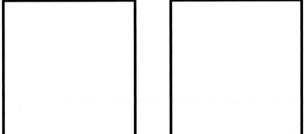

o otter

a antelope

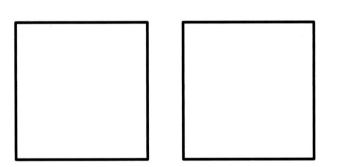

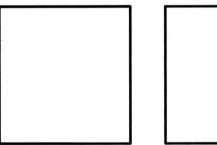

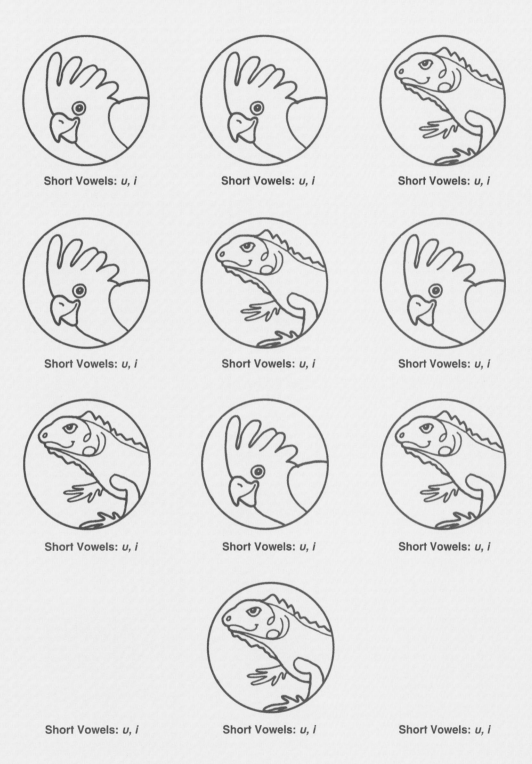

Short Vowels: *u, i*

Short Vowels: *u, i*

Short Vowels: *u, i*

Short Vowels: *u, i*

Short Vowels: *u, i*

Short Vowels: *u, i*

Short Vowels: *u, i*

Short Vowels: *u, i*

Short Vowels: *u, i*

Short Vowels: *u, i*

Short Vowels: *u, i*

Short Vowels: *u, i*

Use these cards with the center mat on page 109.

1. Before using page 109, photocopy page 110 for later use.
2. If desired, laminate the center mat (page 109) and the cards.
3. Cut out the cards.
4. To use, a child turns all the cards full-color side up on a tabletop.

5. The child chooses a picture card and names the picture. She places it near the picture on the mat that has a matching beginning sound. She continues in this way until each space on the center mat is filled.
6. The child names the pictures in each set, listening to confirm that all the pictures begin with the same sound. She flips each card to check her work.

Begins Like Umbrella Cockatoo

Begins Like Iguana

©The Mailbox® • *Sounds Like Fun: Phenomenal Phonics* • TEC60914

Begins Like Iguana or Umbrella Cockatoo

Cut. Glue.

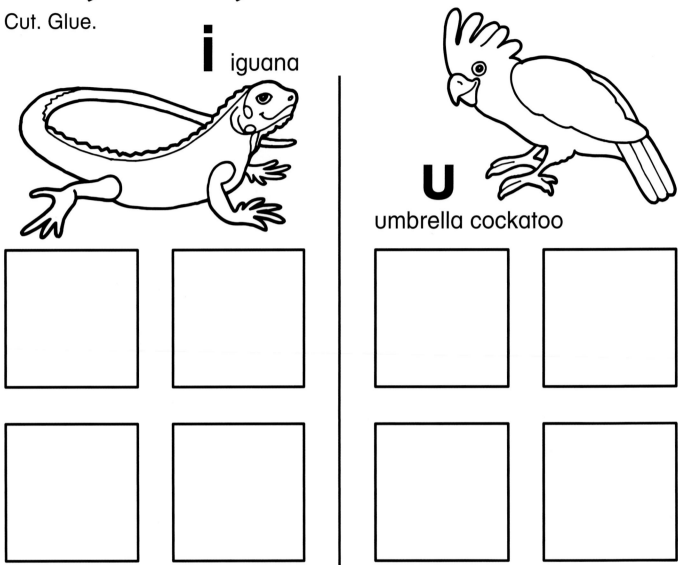

i iguana

U umbrella cockatoo

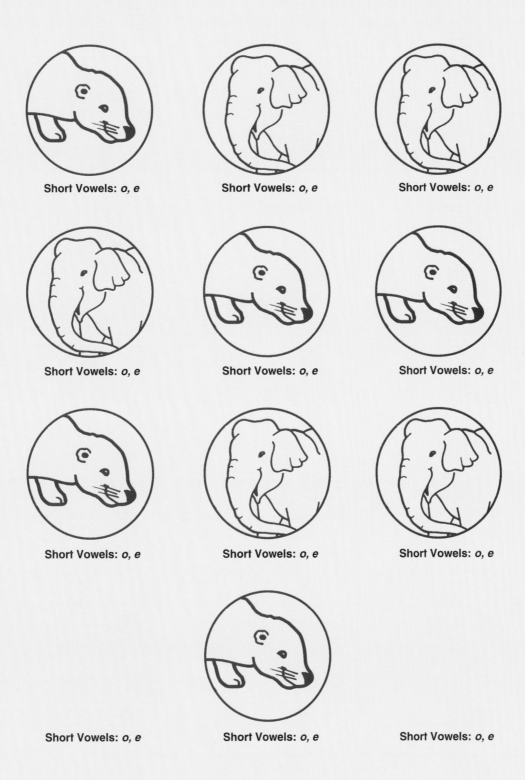

Short Vowels: *o, e*

Short Vowels: *o, e*

Short Vowels: *o, e*

Short Vowels: *o, e*

Short Vowels: *o, e*

Short Vowels: *o, e*

Short Vowels: *o, e*

Short Vowels: *o, e*

Short Vowels: *o, e*

Short Vowels: *o, e*

Short Vowels: *o, e*

Short Vowels: *o, e*

Use these cards with the center mat on page 113.

1. Before using page 113, photocopy page 114 for later use.
2. If desired, laminate the center mat (page 113) and the cards.
3. Cut out the cards.
4. To use, a child turns all the cards full-color side up on a tabletop.
5. The child chooses a picture card and names the picture. He places it near the picture on the mat that has a matching beginning sound. He continues in this way until each space on the center mat is filled.
6. The child names the pictures in each set, listening to confirm that all the pictures begin with the same sound. He flips each card to check his work.

Begins Like Elephant

Begins Like Otter

Begins Like Otter or Elephant

Cut. Glue.

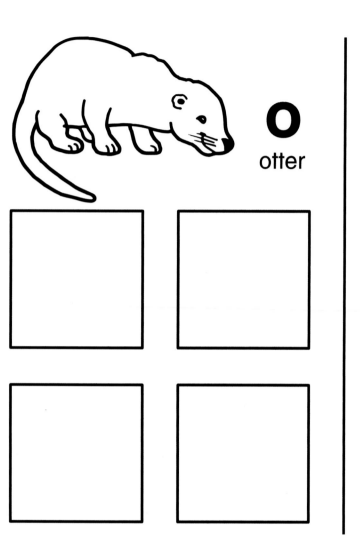

o
otter

e
elephant

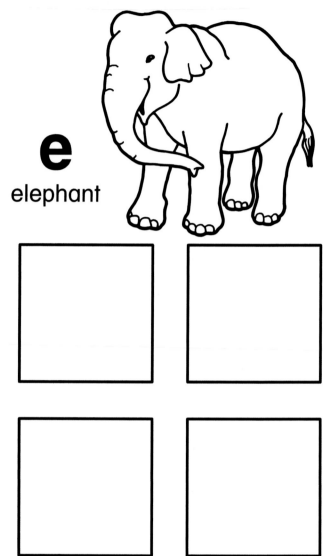

Short Vowels: *a, u*

Short Vowels: *a, u*

Short Vowels: *a, u*

Short Vowels: *a, u*

Short Vowels: *a, u*

Short Vowels: *a, u*

Short Vowels: *a, u*

Short Vowels: *a, u*

Short Vowels: *a, u*

Short Vowels: *a, u*

Short Vowels: *a, u*

Short Vowels: *a, u*

Use these cards with the center mat on page 117.

1. Before using page 117, photocopy page 118 for later use.
2. If desired, laminate the center mat (page 117) and the cards.
3. Cut out the cards.
4. To use, a child turns all the cards full-color side up on a tabletop.
5. The child chooses a picture card and names the picture. She places it near the picture on the mat that has a matching beginning sound. She continues in this way until each space on the center mat is filled.
6. The child names the pictures in each set, listening to confirm that all the pictures begin with the same sound. She flips each card to check her work.

Begins Like Antelope

Begins Like Umbrella Cockatoo

Begins Like Umbrella Cockatoo or Antelope

Cut. Glue.

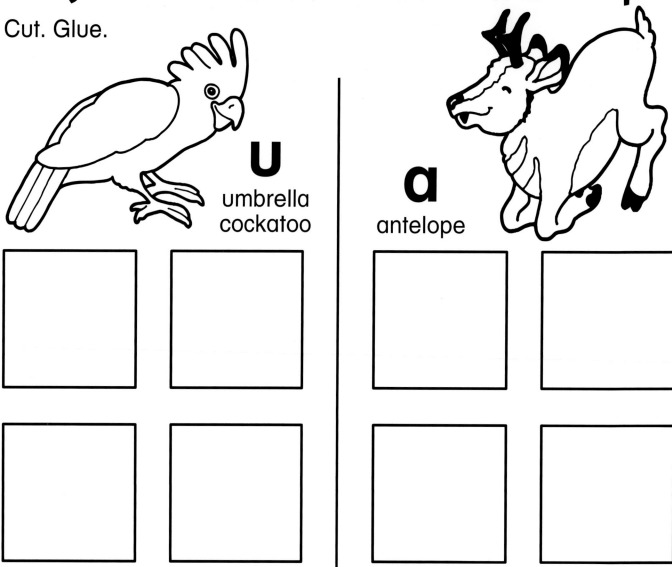

U
umbrella
cockatoo

a
antelope

Long Vowels

Contents

quail

mule

mice

bee

mole

Long Vowel in the Middle

"Hey, Diddle, Diddle" is the inspiration for this hip chant. Before teaching the chant to children, have each child tear a strip of paper into five squares and label each square with a different vowel. Then, as you say the chant and they chime in, have them indicate the long-vowel sound they hear by holding up the corresponding letter during the chant. If desired, extend the chant by continuing to feature different long-vowel words.

Hey, diddle, diddle!
There's a sound in the middle,
A sound inside of _[quail]_. Can you hear?
Hey, diddle, diddle!
[/Ā/] is in the middle.
Listen for [/ā/]. Use your ears!

Repeat the rhyme, making the appropriate substitutions for bee, mice, mole, _and_ mule.

Picture Pairs

Just like the cat and the fiddle, certain animals and objects make perfect pairs! Using photo references if possible, talk about each of these animal names and the animals they represent: _quail, mule, mole, seal, mice._ Assign each child one animal to draw on a large index card. Then have him think of and draw on another index card an object whose name has the same long-vowel sound. Confirm the matching vowel sounds. Next, place the student-drawn card pairs in resealable plastic bags, making sure each bag contains a pair of cards for every vowel. Place the bags at a center. When a student visits the center, he takes a bag and removes an animal card. Then he names the animal and locates the matching long-vowel object card. He continues in this manner until he has matched all the cards in the bag.

Vowels

Hey, Diddle, Diddle Game

This circle-time game makes focusing on long-vowel sounds fun! To prepare, you'll need the card sets from "Picture Pairs" on page 120 and a separate letter card for each of the long vowels. Ensure that for each animal card there is a matching object card. If necessary to make the number of players even, take a card yourself and join in the game. Give one card to each child and help her identify the long-vowel name of the picture. Begin the game by asking students to stand in a circle. Next, hold up a letter card and say, "Hey, diddle, diddle, find your partner in the middle!" Prompt each child who has a matching picture card to hold up her card, move to the center of the circle, and pair up with a partner. Ask each pair of youngsters to say the names of the items on their cards. Then have students return to their places in the circle. Continue with four more rounds of the game, one round for each long-vowel sound. To play additional rounds of the game, have students trade cards.

Making Word Lists

Introduce different ways to spell the same vowel sound with this brainstorming idea. Display a quail picture card near the top of a board or chart. Have children identify the picture and the long-vowel sound. Then challenge youngsters to brainstorm other words that also contain the long *a* sound. Write each suggested word on the board or on a chart. Have students examine the words to determine that there are several ways to spell the long *a* sound *(a_e, ai, ay)*. Use colorful chalk or a marker to trace over the spellings children point out. Repeat the activity for different vowels as time permits.

cake rail hay
snake pail play
tale paint

Long Vowels

Word-Sorting Center

This center idea reinforces long-vowel sounds and supports spelling skills. Display a student-drawn quail card in the top row of your pocket chart. Place the pocket chart in a center along with word cards containing several spellings for the long *a* sound. To use the center, invite a child to display the word cards in rows according to the different ways to spell the long *a* sound. Later, replace the cards at the center with an animal picture card whose name contains a different long-vowel sound and word cards that feature different spellings for the sound.

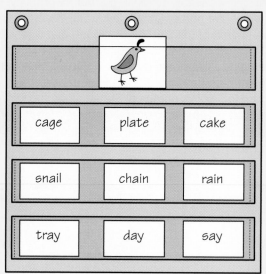

Word Workshop

Transparencies are just the ticket for group practice in spelling long vowels. To prepare for several workshops, make transparencies of the center mats on pages 129, 133, 137, 141, 145, 149, and 153. To use the first transparency, ask half of your students to think of long *a* words with the same vowel spelling as *quail* and ask the other half to think of long *a* words with the same vowel spelling as *cage*. Project the transparency of page 129. Encourage each group to take turns suggesting a word that's spelled like its key word. Write suggested words on the transparency, one word per box, until each team has filled its boxes. To increase the challenge, ask for two or three words per box. Review the words listed and help students make observations about the words in each list before ending the activity. On another day, repeat the process to emphasize other spellings or other vowels by similarly using one of the other transparencies you prepared.

Long Vowels: *o, u*

Long Vowels: *o, u*

Long Vowels: *o, u*

Long Vowels: *o, u*

Long Vowels: *o, u*

Long Vowels: *o, u*

cube

Long Vowels: *o, u*

tube

Long Vowels: *o, u*

mule

Long Vowels: *o, u*

bone

Long Vowels: *o, u*

rose

Long Vowels: *o, u*

hose

Long Vowels: *o, u*

Use these cards with the center mat on page 125.

1. Before using page 125, photocopy page 126 for later use.
2. If desired, laminate the center mat (page 125) and the cards. Cut out the cards.
3. To use, a child turns all the cards blue side up on a tabletop and separates the picture cards from the word cards.
4. The child names a picture card and places it beneath the picture on the mat whose name has a matching long-vowel sound. He continues in this way until each picture is placed.
5. He uses his letter-sound knowledge to match a word card to each picture.
6. The child names the pictures and reads the words in each set, listening to confirm that all the pictures in each set have the same long-vowel sound. He flips each card to check his work.

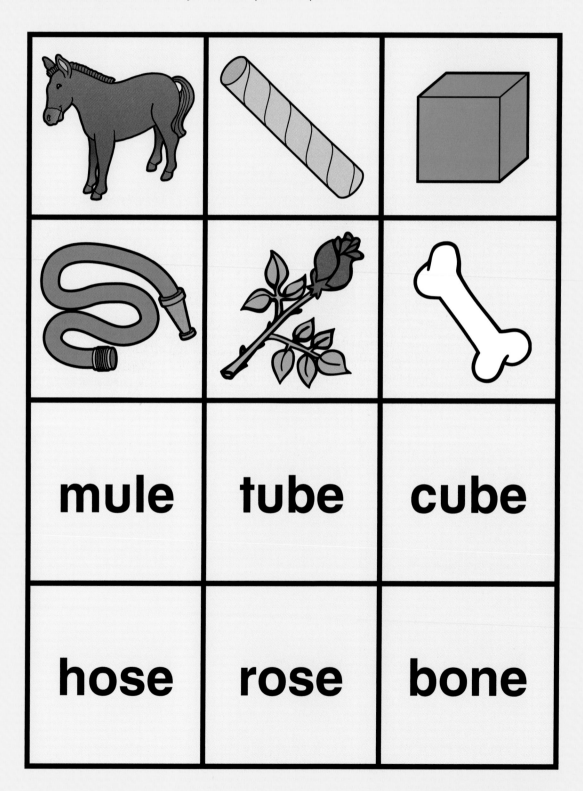

| mule | tube | cube |
| hose | rose | bone |

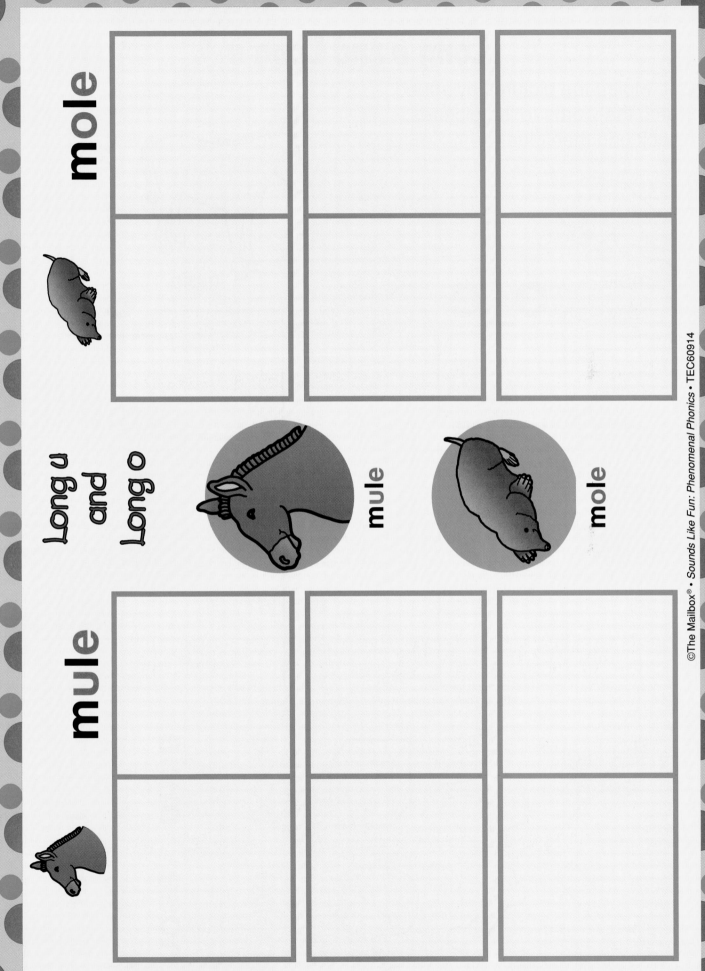

mole

mule

Long u
and
Long o

mule

mole

Long *o* and Long *u*

Cut. Match the pictures by sound.
Match the words to the pictures.
Check and then glue.

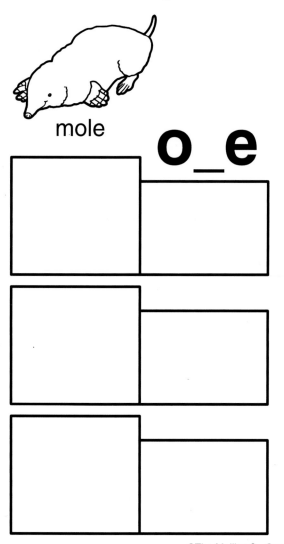

mole

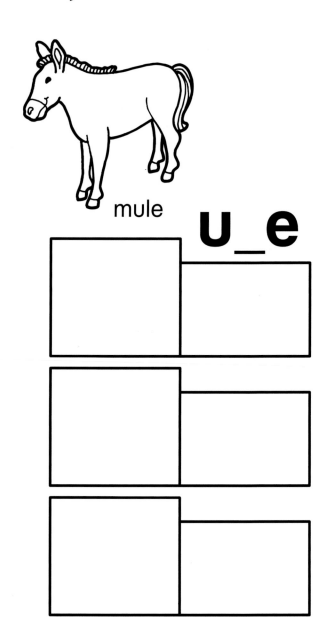

mule

o_e

u_e

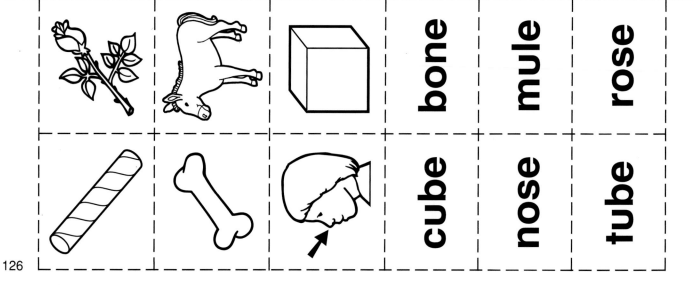

bone   mule   rose

cube   nose   tube

Spellings: *ai, a_e*   Spellings: *ai, a_e*   Spellings: *ai, a_e*

Spellings: *ai, a_e*   Spellings: *ai, a_e*   Spellings: *ai, a_e*

train   chain   nail

Spellings: *ai, a_e*   Spellings: *ai, a_e*   Spellings: *ai, a_e*

tape   cake   rake

Spellings: *ai, a_e*   Spellings: *ai, a_e*   Spellings: *ai, a_e*

Use these cards with the center mat on page 129.

1. Before using page 129, photocopy page 130 for later use.
2. If desired, laminate the center mat (page 129) and the cards. Cut out the cards.
3. To use, a child turns all the cards blue side up on a tabletop, separates the picture cards from the word cards, and moves the word cards momentarily out of view.

4. The child names a picture card and places it beneath the picture on the mat whose name shares the same spelling for the long *a* sound. She may use a pencil and scrap paper to try out possible spellings of the word. She continues in this way until each picture is placed.
5. Then she matches a word card to each picture.
6. The child examines each picture-word set to determine whether the cards are correctly placed. She then flips the cards to check her work.

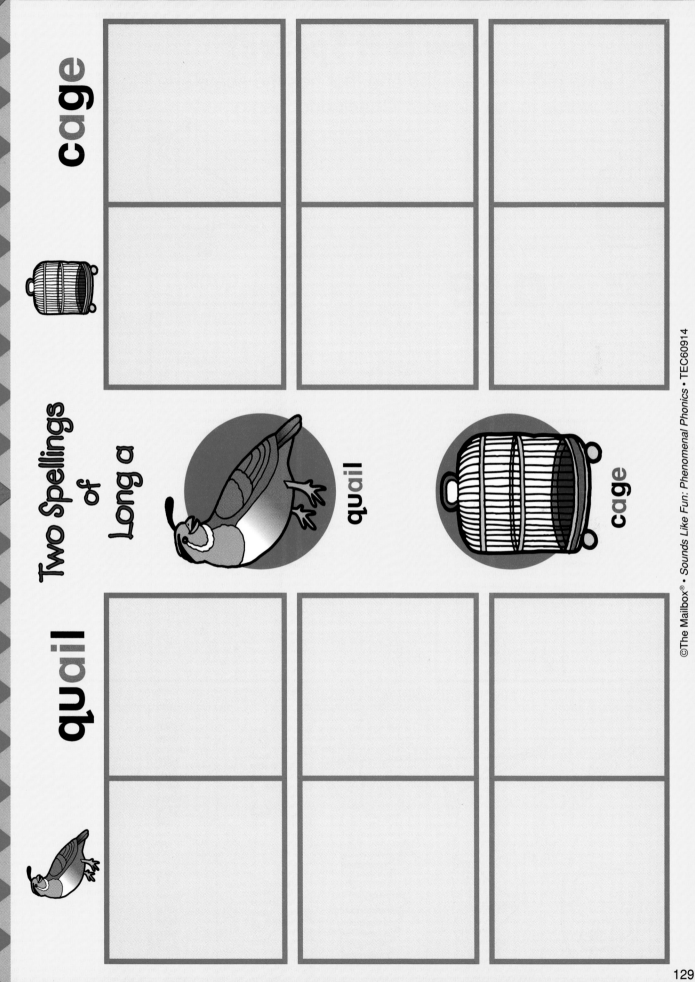

cage

quail

Two Spellings
of
Long a

quail

cage

How Is It Spelled?

Cut. Put each picture below the one that has the same spelling of long *a*.
Match the words to the pictures. Check and then glue.

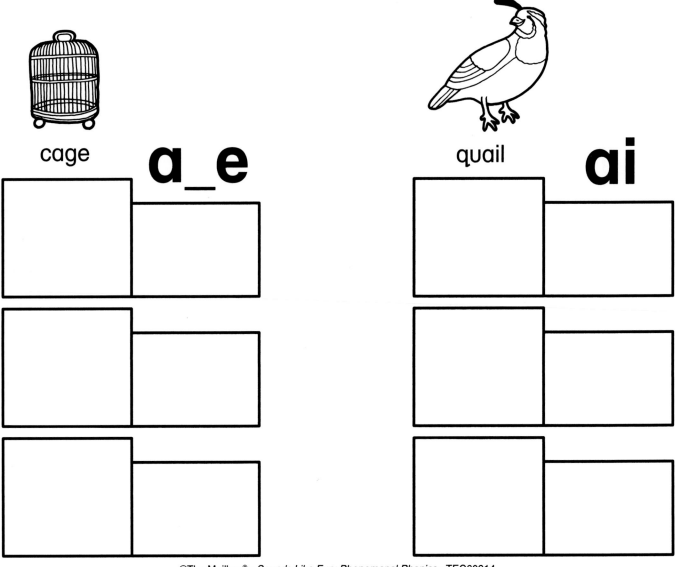

cage **a_e**

quail **ai**

cake | chain | rake

rain | gate | sail

Spellings: *ai, ay*

Spellings: *ai, ay*

Spellings: *ai, ay*

Spellings: *ai, ay*

Spellings: *ai, ay*

Spellings: *ai, ay*

X-ray

Spellings: *ai, ay*

gray

Spellings: *ai, ay*

tray

Spellings: *ai, ay*

rain

Spellings: *ai, ay*

snail

Spellings: *ai, ay*

paint

Spellings: *ai, ay*

Use these cards with the center mat on page 133.

1. Before using page 133, photocopy page 134 for later use.
2. If desired, laminate the center mat (page 133) and the cards. Cut out the cards.
3. To use, a child turns all the cards blue side up on a tabletop, separates the picture cards from the word cards, and moves the word cards momentarily out of view.
4. The child names a picture card and places it beneath the picture on the mat whose name shares the same spelling for the long *a* sound. He may use a pencil and scrap paper to try out possible spellings of the word. He continues in this way until each picture is placed.
5. Then he matches a word card to each picture.
6. The child examines each picture-word set to determine whether the cards are correctly placed. He then flips the cards to check his work.

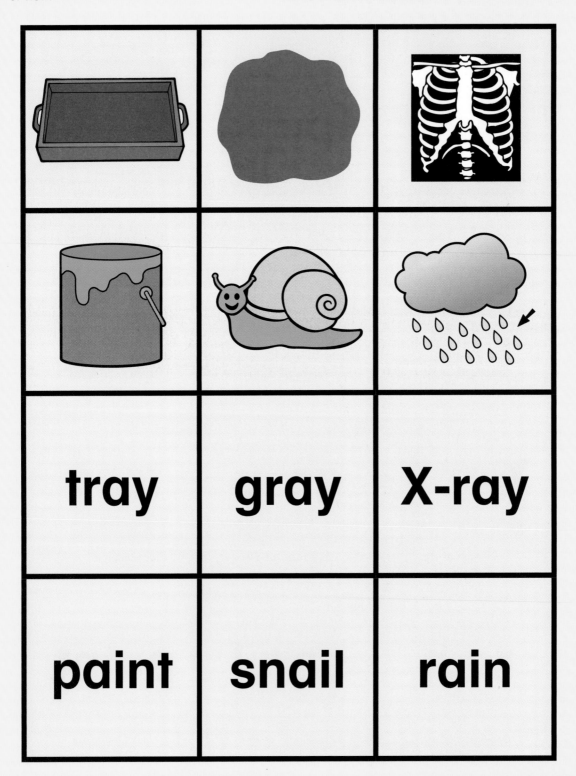

tray   gray   X-ray

paint   snail   rain

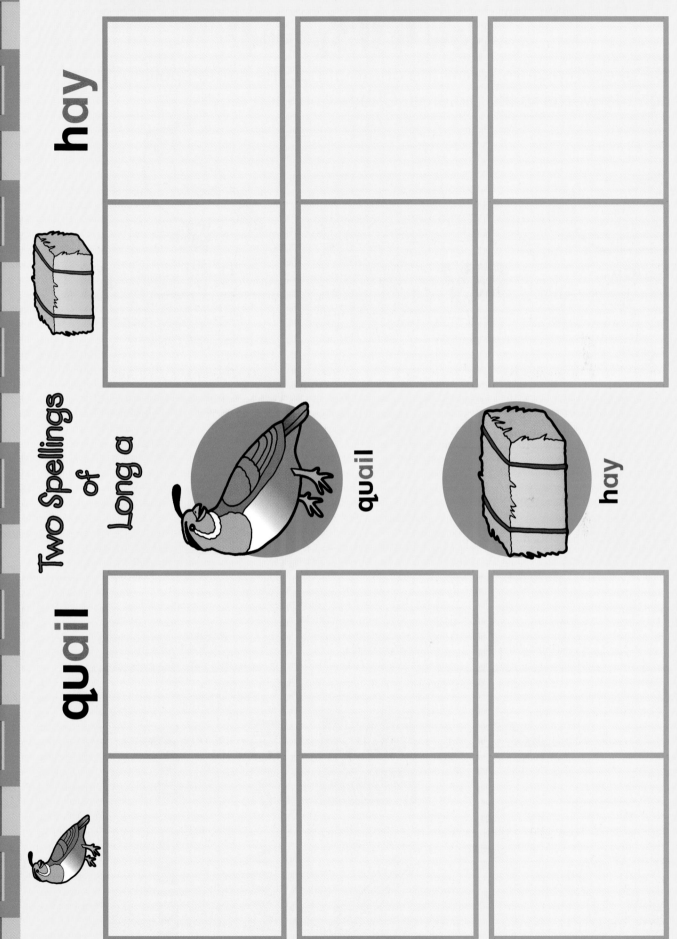

hay

Two Spellings
of
Long a

quail

hay

quail

How Is It Spelled?

Cut. Put each picture below the one that has the same spelling of long *a*.
Match the words to the pictures. Check and then glue.

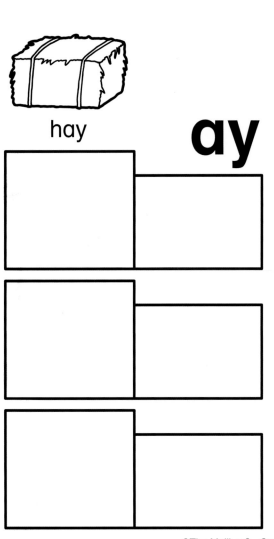

hay **ay**

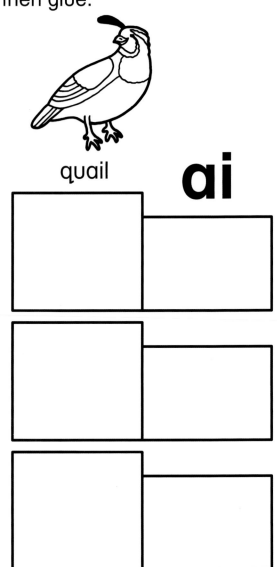

quail **ai**

©The Mailbox® • *Sounds Like Fun: Phenomenal Phonics* • TEC60914

snail

tray

chain

spray

rain

X-ray

Spellings: *ea, ee*

Spellings: *ea, ee*

Spellings: *ea, ee*

Spellings: *ea, ee*

Spellings: *ea, ee*

Spellings: *ea, ee*

jeep

Spellings: *ea, ee*

three

Spellings: *ea, ee*

beach

Spellings: *ea, ee*

sheep

Spellings: *ea, ee*

bead

Spellings: *ea, ee*

seal

Spellings: *ea, ee*

Use these cards with the center mat on page 137.

1. Before using page 137, photocopy page 138 for later use.
2. If desired, laminate the center mat (page 137) and the cards. Cut out the cards.
3. To use, a child turns all the cards blue side up on a tabletop, separates the picture cards from the word cards, and moves the word cards momentarily out of view.
4. The child names a picture card and places it beneath the picture on the mat whose name shares the same spelling for the long *e* sound. She may use a pencil and scrap paper to try out possible spellings of the word. She continues in this way until each picture is placed.
5. Then she matches a word card to each picture.
6. The child examines each picture-word set to determine whether the cards are correctly placed. She then flips the cards to check her work.

bee

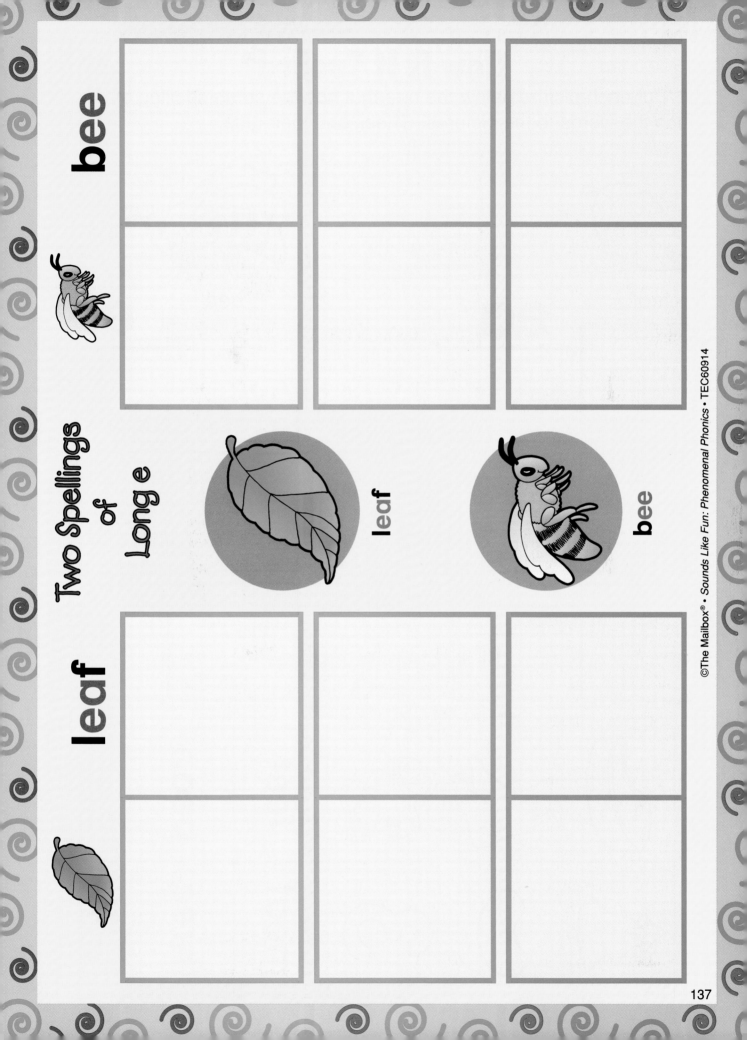

Two Spellings of Long e

leaf

bee

leaf

How Is It Spelled?

Cut. Put each picture below the one that has the same spelling of long *e*.
Match the words to the pictures. Check and then glue.

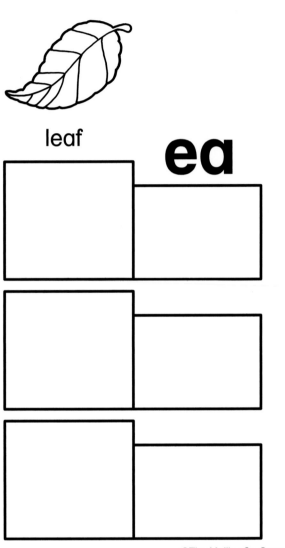

leaf **ea**

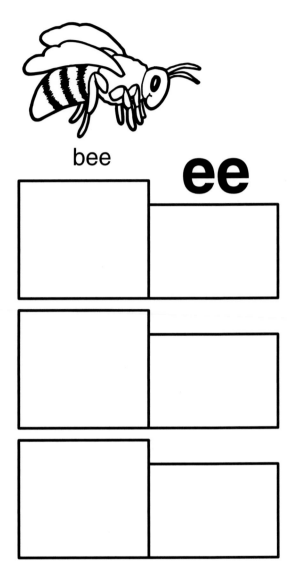

bee **ee**

©The Mailbox® • *Sounds Like Fun: Phenomenal Phonics* • TEC60914

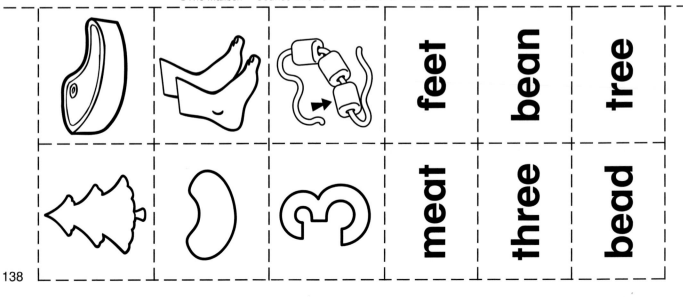

138

Spellings: *y, i_e*

Spellings: *y, i_e*

Spellings: *y, i_e*

Spellings: *y, i_e*

Spellings: *y, i_e*

Spellings: *y, i_e*

slide

Spellings: *y, i_e*

dime

Spellings: *y, i_e*

bike

Spellings: *y, i_e*

fry

Spellings: *y, i_e*

cry

Spellings: *y, i_e*

fly

Spellings: *y, i_e*

Use these cards with the center mat on page 141.

1. Before using page 141, photocopy page 142 for later use.
2. If desired, laminate the center mat (page 141) and the cards. Cut out the cards.
3. To use, a child turns all the cards blue side up on a tabletop, separates the picture cards from the word cards, and moves the word cards momentarily out of view.
4. The child names a picture card and places it beneath the picture on the mat whose name shares the same spelling for the long *i* sound. She may use a pencil and scrap paper to try out possible spellings of the word. She continues in this way until each picture is placed.
5. Then she matches a word card to each picture.
6. The child examines each picture-word set to determine whether the cards are correctly placed. She then flips the cards to check her work.

bike	**dime**	**slide**
fly	**cry**	**fry**

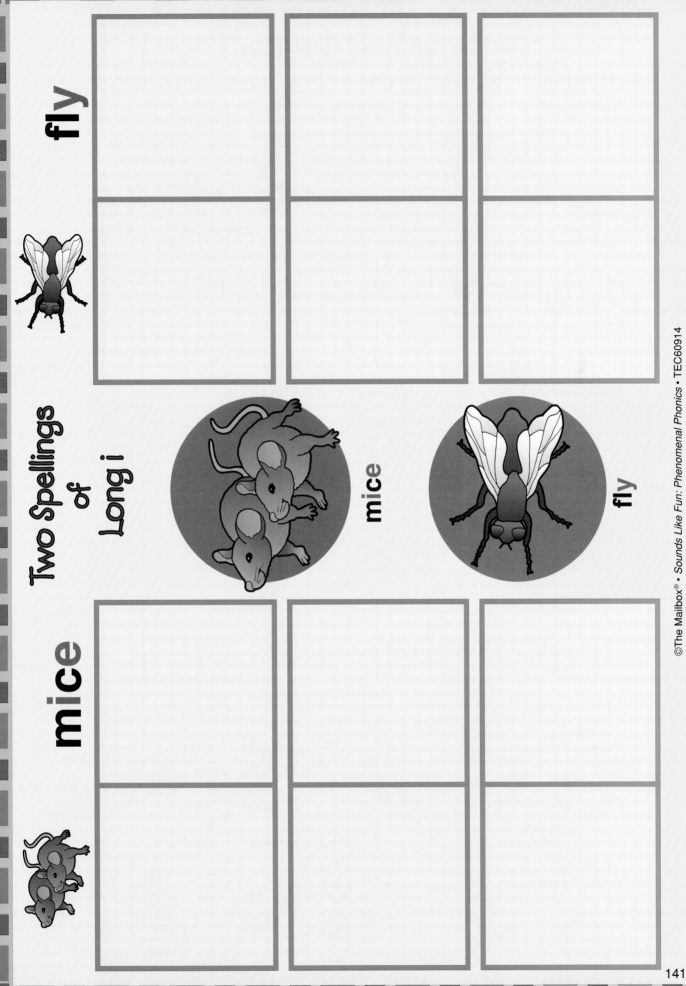

fly

Two Spellings of Long i

mice

mice

fly

How Is It Spelled?

Cut. Put each picture below the one that has the same spelling of long *i*.
Match the words to the pictures. Check and then glue.

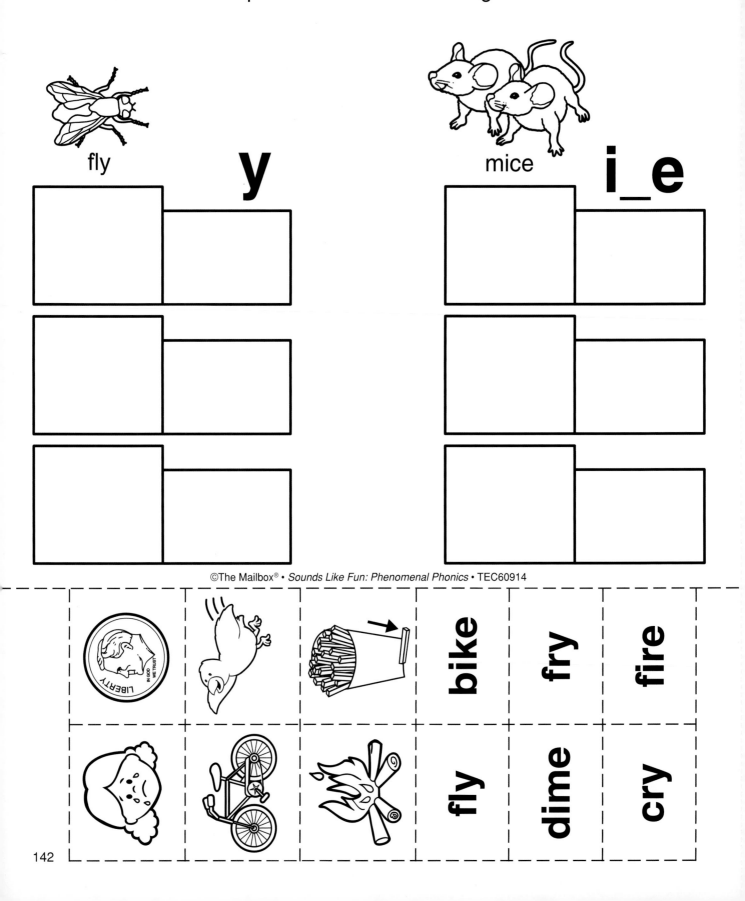

fly   **y**

mice   **i_e**

©The Mailbox® • *Sounds Like Fun: Phenomenal Phonics* • TEC60914

bike   fry   fire

fly   dime   cry

Spellings: *i_e, igh*

Spellings: *i_e, igh*

Spellings: *i_e, igh*

Spellings: *i_e, igh*

Spellings: *i_e, igh*

Spellings: *i_e, igh*

kite

Spellings: *i_e, igh*

nine

Spellings: *i_e, igh*

dice

Spellings: *i_e, igh*

night

Spellings: *i_e, igh*

fight

Spellings: *i_e, igh*

light

Spellings: *i_e, igh*

Use these cards with the center mat on page 145.

1. Before using page 145, photocopy page 146 for later use.
2. If desired, laminate the center mat (page 145) and the cards. Cut out the cards.
3. To use, a child turns all the cards blue side up on a tabletop, separates the picture cards from the word cards, and moves the word cards momentarily out of view.
4. The child names a picture card and places it beneath the picture on the mat whose name shares the same spelling for the long *i* sound. He may use a pencil and scrap paper to try out possible spellings of the word. He continues in this way until each picture is placed.
5. Then he matches a word card to each picture.
6. The child examines each picture-word set to determine whether the cards are correctly placed. He then flips the cards to check his work.

dice | nine | kite

light | fight | night

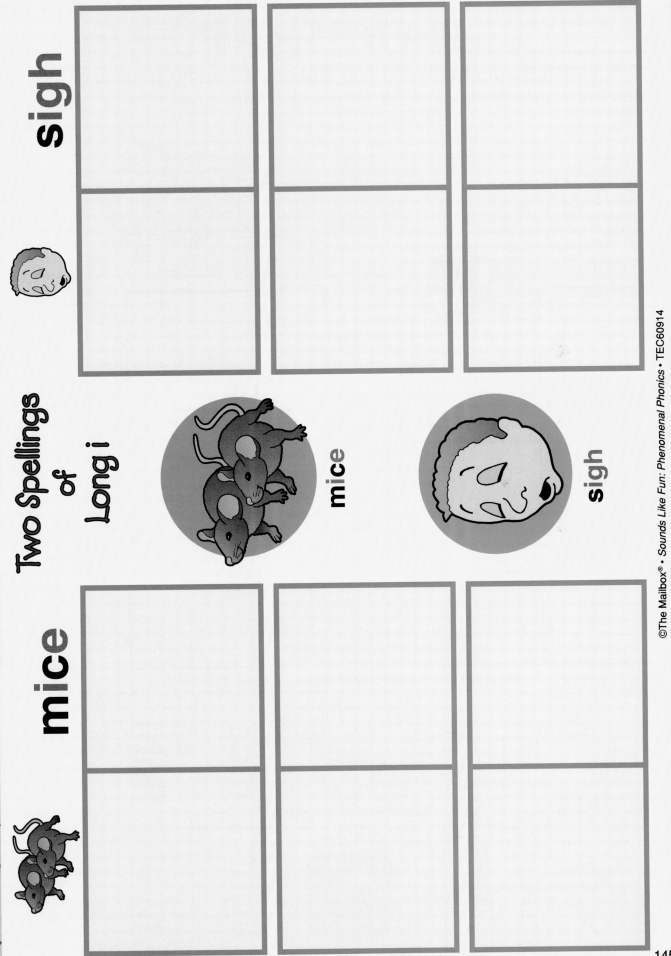

Two Spellings
of
Long i

mice

sigh

mice

sigh

How Is It Spelled?

Cut. Put each picture below the one that has the same spelling of long *i*. Match the words to the pictures. Check and then glue.

sigh **igh**

mice **i_e**

dice

fight

kite

light

five

night

Spellings: *o_e, ow*

Spellings: *o_e, ow*

Spellings: *o_e, ow*

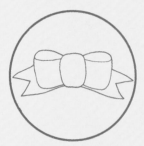

Spellings: *o_e, ow*

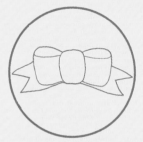

Spellings: *o_e, ow*

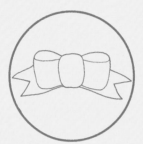

Spellings: *o_e, ow*

rope

Spellings: *o_e, ow*

bone

Spellings: *o_e, ow*

nose

Spellings: *o_e, ow*

throw

Spellings: *o_e, ow*

snow

Spellings: *o_e, ow*

bowl

Spellings: *o_e, ow*

Use these cards with the center mat on page 149.

1. Before using page 149, photocopy page 150 for later use.
2. If desired, laminate the center mat (page 149) and the cards. Cut out the cards.
3. To use, a child turns all the cards blue side up on a tabletop, separates the picture cards from the word cards, and moves the word cards momentarily out of view.
4. The child names a picture card and places it beneath the picture on the mat whose name shares the same spelling for the long *o* sound. She may use a pencil and scrap paper to try out possible spellings of the word. She continues in this way until each picture is placed.
5. Then she matches a word card to each picture.
6. The child examines each picture-word set to determine whether the cards are correctly placed. She then flips the cards to check her work.

nose   bone   rope

bowl   snow   throw

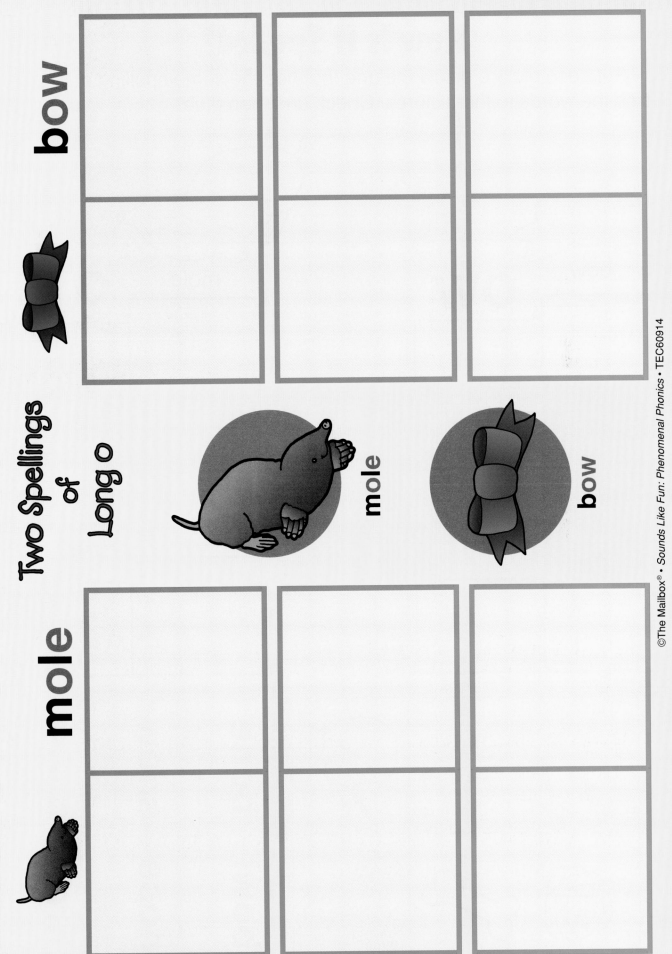

bow

mole

Two Spellings of Long o

mole

bow

How Is It Spelled?

Cut. Put each picture below the one that has the same spelling of long *o*.
Match the words to the pictures. Check and then glue.

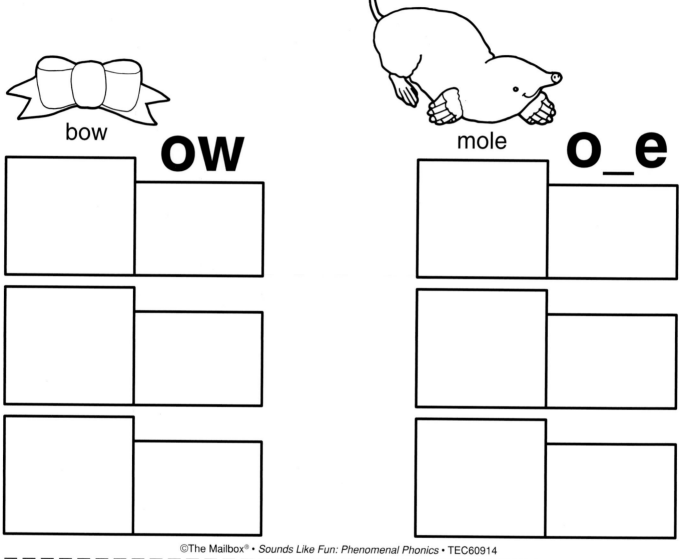

bow

ow

mole

o_e

bone   snow   rope

bowl   nose   throw

Spellings: *oa, ow*

Spellings: *oa, ow*

Spellings: *oa, ow*

Spellings: *oa, ow*

Spellings: *oa, ow*

Spellings: *oa, ow*

throw

Spellings: *oa, ow*

bowl

Spellings: *oa, ow*

crow

Spellings: *oa, ow*

soap

Spellings: *oa, ow*

boat

Spellings: *oa, ow*

road

Spellings: *oa, ow*

Use these cards with the center mat on page 153.

1. Before using page 153, photocopy page 154 for later use.
2. If desired, laminate the center mat (page 153) and the cards. Cut out the cards.
3. To use, a child turns all the cards blue side up on a tabletop, separates the picture cards from the word cards, and moves the word cards momentarily out of view.
4. The child names a picture card and places it beneath the picture on the mat whose name shares the same spelling for the long *o* sound. He may use a pencil and scrap paper to try out possible spellings of the word. He continues in this way until each picture is placed.
5. Then he matches a word card to each picture.
6. The child examines each picture-word set to determine whether the cards are correctly placed. He then flips the cards to check his work.

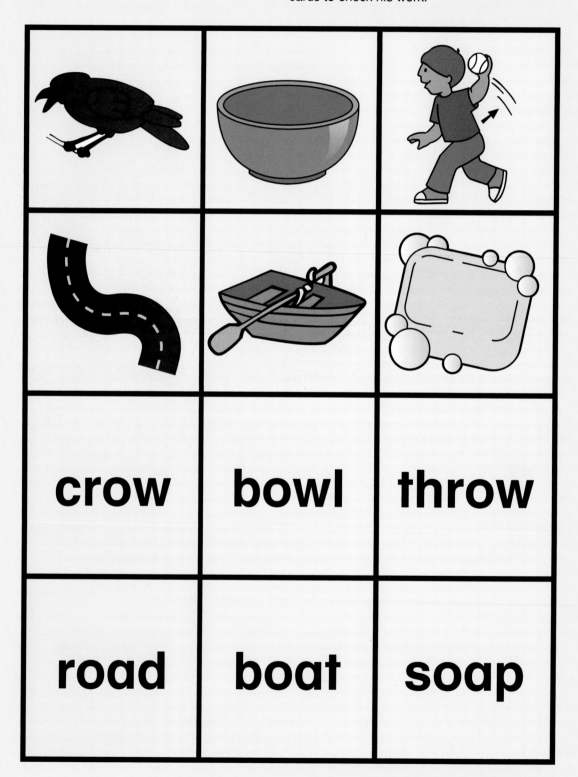

| crow | bowl | throw |
| road | boat | soap |

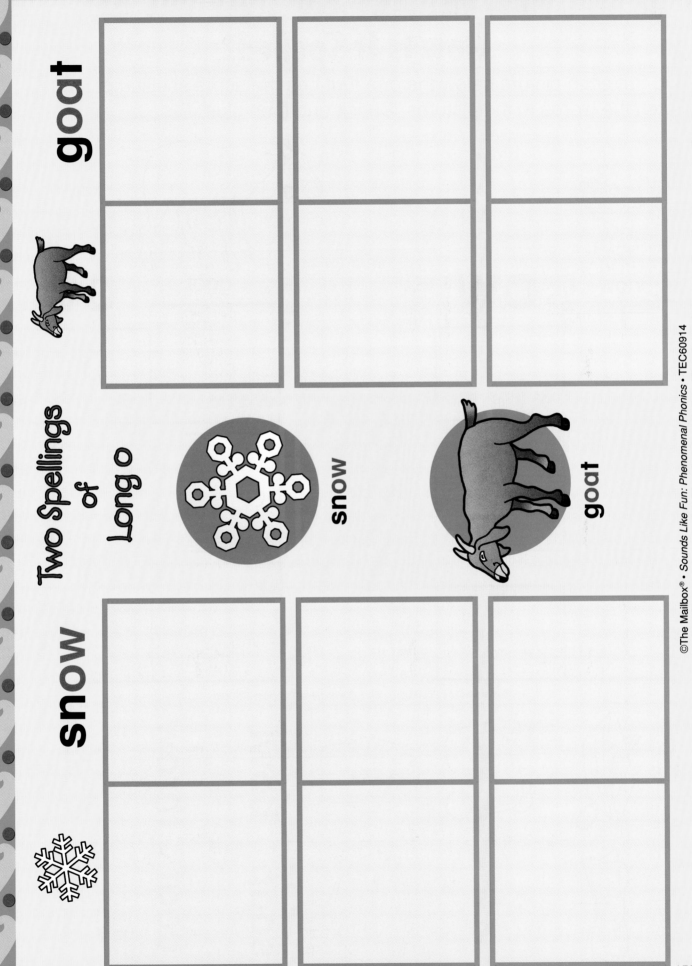

goat

Two Spellings of Long o

snow

snow

goat

snow

How Is It Spelled?

Cut. Put each picture below the one that has the same spelling of long *o*. Match the words to the pictures. Check and then glue.

snow **ow**

goat **oa**

bowl

throw

boat

soap

coat

bow

Adaptable Miniposters

This section contains blend, word family, and long-vowel miniposters. Copy them, cut them apart, and use them over and over to promote growth in letter-sound association, word recognition, and spelling.

Some ways to use the miniposters are

- as display cards **when introducing a blend, word family, or long-vowel spelling**

- as labels for a **word wall**

- as **covers for booklets** containing collections of related words

skunk

sk

swan

sw

snake

sn

sp

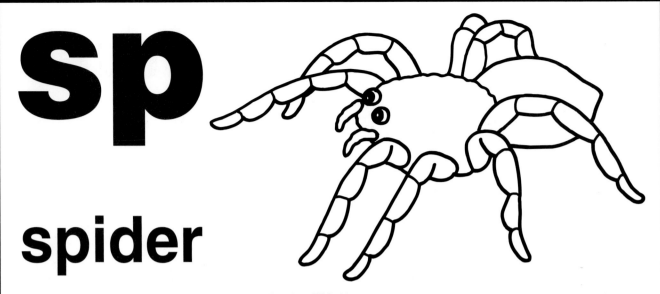

spider

stork

st

blue jay

bl

clown fish

cl

flamingo

fl

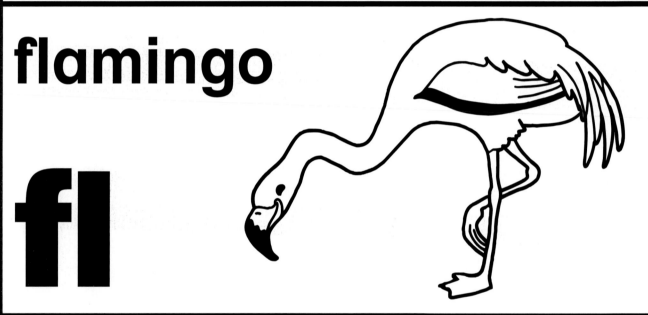

crab

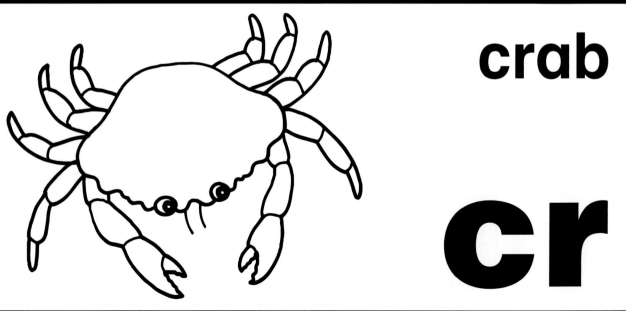

cr

dragon

dr

frog

fr

cat

at

ag

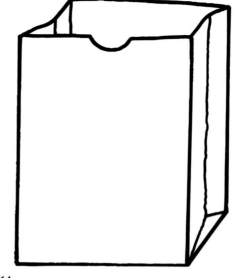

bag

can

an

ram

am

ig
pig

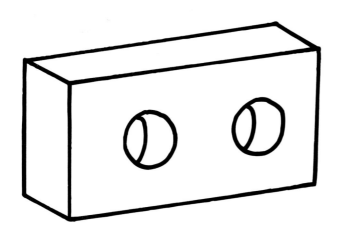

brick

ick

sit

it

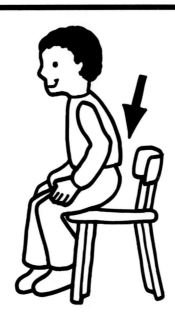

og

dog

op

mop

pot

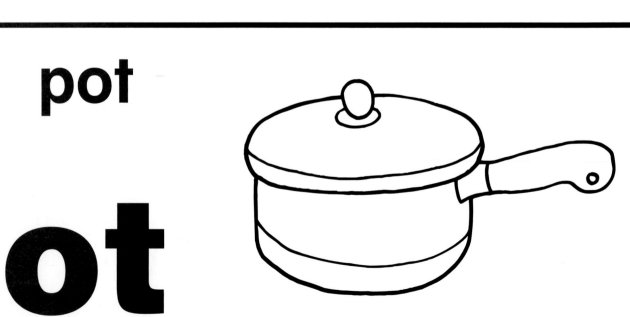

ot

hen

en

bed

ed

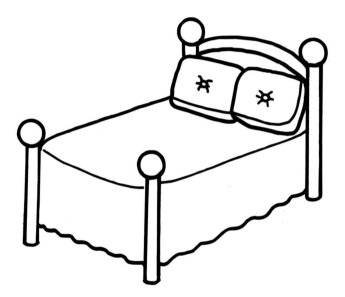

bell

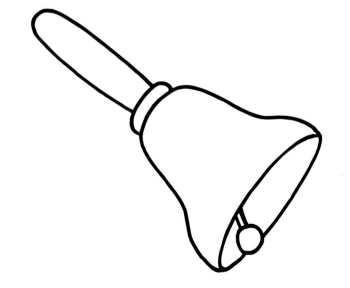

ell

ug

rug

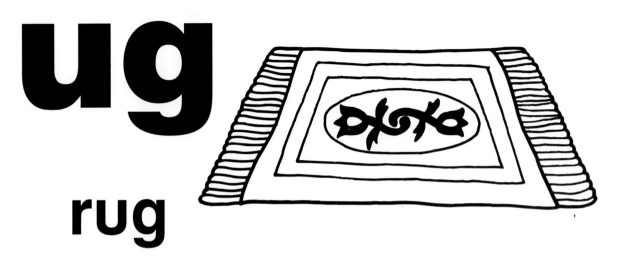

tub

ub

duck

uck

cake

a_e

quail

ai

ay

tray

bee

ee

seal

ea

igh

sigh

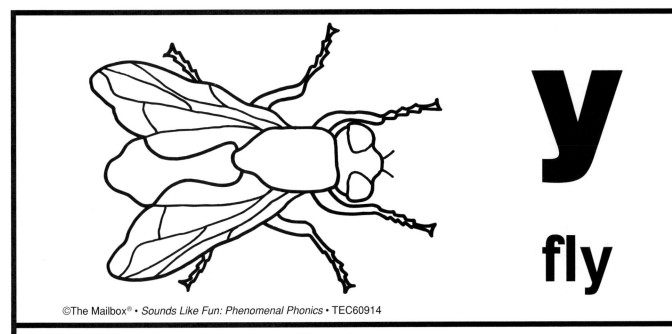

y

fly

mice

i_e

mole

o_e

bow

ow

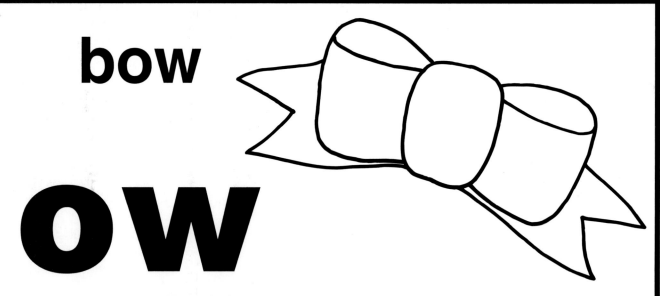

goat

oa

mule

u_e